AF803355

EARLY MACKINAC

A SKETCH

HISTORICAL AND DESCRIPTIVE

BY

MEADE C. WILLIAMS

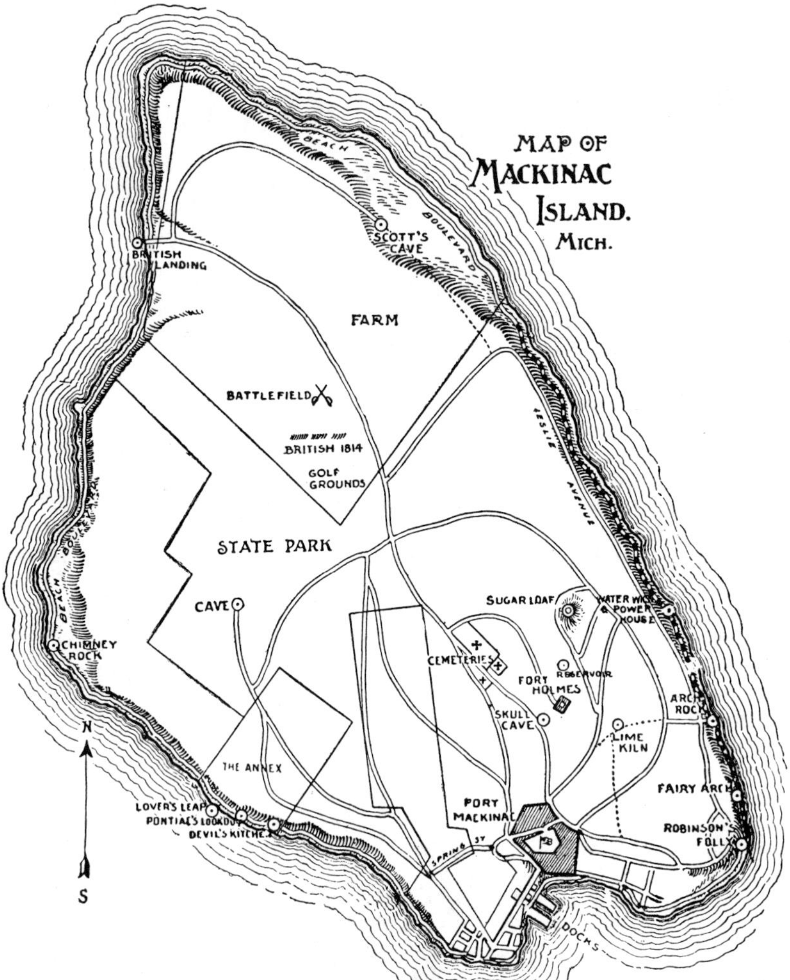
MAP OF
MACKINAC
ISLAND.
MICH.
BEACH
SCOTT'S CAVE
BOULEVARD
BRITISH LANDING
FARM
BATTLEFIELD
BRITISH 1814
GOLF GROUNDS
LESLIE AVENUE
STATE PARK
CAVE
SUGAR LOAF
WATER WKS & POWER HOUSE
CEMETERIES
RESERVOIR
FORT HOLMES
CHIMNEY ROCK
BEACH
SKULL CAVE
ARCH ROCK
LIME KILN
THE ANNEX
FAIRY ARCH
FORT MACKINAC
LOVER'S LEAP
PONTIAC'S LOOKOUT
DEVIL'S KITCHEN
ROBINSON'S FOLLY
SPRING ST
DOCKS
N
S

EARLY MACKINAC
A Sketch
Historical and Descriptive
By
Meade C. Williams

Introductory Essay
by
Larry Massie
Allegan, Michigan
1986

Published
by
Avery Color Studios
Au Train, Michigan 49806

Library of Congress Number Pending
ISBN 0-932212-49-2

First Edition Printed March 1987
Reprinted - 1992

EARLY MACKINAC was first published in 1897, revised in 1901 and 1912.

I know an isle, an emerald set in pearl,
  Mounting the chain of topaz, amethyst,
That forms the circle of our summer seas —
  The fairest that our western sun hath kissed.

For all things lovely lend her loveliness;
  The waves reach forth white fingers to caress,
The four winds, murmuringly meet to woo
  And cloudless skies bend in blue tenderness.

The classic nymphs still haunt her grassy pools;
  Her woods, in green, the Norseland elves have draped,
And fairies, from all lands, or far or near,
  Her airy cliffs, and carving shores, have shaped.

Of old, strange suitors came in quest of her,
  Some in the pride of conquest, some for pelf;
Priests in their piety, red men for revenge —
  All seek her now, alone, for her fair self.

Rev. David H. Riddle.

TO ALL THOSE

WHO HAVING ONCE KNOWN

THE ISLAND OF THE STRAITS

STILL REMEMBER ITS CHARM,

AND REMAIN UNDER THE POWER OF ITS SPELL,

THIS BOOK IS DEDICATED.

THE GRIFFIN — FIRST SAIL VESSEL ON THE LAKES.

Built by La Salle, on Niagara River a few miles above the Falls, in 1678–79, and named in allusion to the arms of his friend, Count de Frontenac, in which griffins figured. Set sail August 7, 1679 — La Salle her commander and Hennepin the journalist of the expedition. This was the first voyage ever made by Europeans on these inland seas. Arrived in the Straits August 27th, at what is now St. Ignace of the northern mainland, four miles across from the island of Mackinac. Anchored in a bay overlooked by two rocky bluffs, known in Indian tradition as the He and She Rabbit. The former also known as Sitting Rabbit, or Rabbit's Back. The Indians were greatly amazed to see a ship in their country, and to hear the sound of its cannon. Hennepin says, "In this bay where the Griffin was riding we looked with pleasure at this large, well-equipped vessel amid a hundred or a hundred and twenty bark canoes coming and going from taking white fish which these Indians catch with nets." Leaving the Straits the party set out on Lake Michigan and sailed as far west and south as Green Bay. Here La Salle sent back the Griffin, loaded with furs and bound for Niagara. The vessel was lost, with all on board — it is thought in the northern part of Lake Michigan and thus perhaps not far from the Mackinac region.

PREFACE OF FORMER EDITION

This book by my father came from an affectionate interest in the place where he spent many of the happiest summers of his life, and where, while planning another and larger book about this historically romantic region, he died in the summer of 1906.

Even those on the cool deck of the passing steamer, who merely look at the quaint 18th century fort exquisitely placed upon the hill overlooking the crescent harbor, must feel the charm of this vividly green island with the pure white beach sharply cutting the brilliantly blue waters of the Straits of Mackinac.

But my father's feeling went deeper than æsthetics. His devotion was more like the love of place shown in the sentiment for ancestral landmarks. He began his annual sojournings many years ago, before the days of garish hotels and cheap excursions. With occasional interruptions for travel he remained faithful, even after the island was pronounced "spoiled" by many of his friends among the original summer colony. So he knew the old inhabitants, all of them. He was a friend — a generous friend, we learned afterwards — to the fast disappearing Indians and the half-breeds who carried in their veins the blood of some of the oldest families of France, as was betrayed by their names. From them he picked up Indian tales, gathered local traditions of the French, Indian and English wars, and collected stories about the "good old days" when Mackinac was the headquarters of the John Jacob Astor fur trade. Most of all, he became an expert in the stirring history of the Indian missions. He led in the restoration of the old mission church on the island — and insisted upon keeping the old gray weathered boards free from modern paint! . . .

In this way he began gathering, for his own delectation and the entertainment of family friends, lore and legend which were perhaps on the verge of oblivion. In this way his romantic and historical interest kept increasing until it became a passionate hobby, for which he was often joked at the dinner table. He bought many books, took journeys to distant libraries, and, in short, became somewhat of an authority upon this interesting chapter of American history.

The following pages are the result. They were written originally for private circulation, but when printed as a book it at once became so popular that new editions — with revised and added chapters — were demanded every season. This was very pleasing to my father.

JESSE LYNCH WILLIAMS.

Washington Road
Princeton, N. J.

PREFACE EARLIER EDITION

This book was first issued in 1897. My thirteen summers at Mackinac Island up to that date have since increased to sixteen. I have felt moved from my acquaintance with the Island and my interest in it, to furnish in written form some of its history.

The book now enters its third edition. It is very considerably enlarged over the first and second issues.

While it is believed this portrayal in its historical portion may have interest for the general reader, it at the same time carries a local coloring which may more particularly appeal to those who know the place and who visit its shores. As the charm of the locality is due, in no small degree, to the halo of antiquity which hangs over it, I have felt warranted in giving special (though not exclusive) attention to *early* Mackinac.

The work embodies the result of no little research and investigation. As the reader will perceive, I am much indebted to the various writings of Henry R. Schoolcraft who dwelt for twenty years in the upper lakes region, and for eight years of this time was a resident of the Island. I also express my obligations to the valuable series of "Collections and Researches," a work carried on by the Michigan Pioneer and Historical Society. These collections at present number twenty-eight volumes. The use they make of the important "Haldimand Papers," of Canada, bring to hand much of the early military history of the Straits and of the Island fort.

St. Louis, Mo. *Mackinac Island.*
June, 1901.

CONTENTS

CONTENTS

CONTENTS

ILLUSTRATIONS

INTRODUCTION

The Literature of the Mackinac Country

With the exception of Sault Ste. Marie, no other Michigan place possesses so rich and colorful a heritage as Mackinac Island and the region of the straits. Few midwestern sites have so captured the enthusiasm of authors. A diversity of printed sources extending from the 17th century to the present document and celebrate this romantic area.

Journals penned by early explorers preserve original impressions. Excursionists captured the region's beauty in published travel narratives, and residents recorded their experiences in autobiographies. Beginning in the 1790's Mackinac Island inspired scores of poets and novelists as a setting for fictional writings. The island produced William Beaumont's classical treatise, which revolutionized medical thought, and was the site of much of Henry Schoolcraft's monumental ethnographical work. Jesse James Strang, King of Beaver Island, penned the first history of Michilimackinac and the adjoining territory in 1854, and each succeeding generation contributed its own version of the past.

In 1897, Meade C. Williams produced a slim volume of 111 pages entitled *Early Mackinac: "The Fairy Island"*. Based on an extensive study of the literature of the island, Williams' book and his later revised edition would become some of the most popular general accounts of the island's history. Williams had first come to Mackinac Island in 1884, soon became enamored with its history, and each season passionately collected new sources and interviewed early residents.

The Rev. Williams, long a trustee of the old Mission Church, led a campaign to restore the structure. He first ventured into print in 1895 with a 22 page historical discourse, *The Old Mission Church of Mackinac Island,* printed in Detroit by the Wilton-Smith Company. Two years later Williams chose the St. Louis publishing firm of Bushart Brothers for the first edition of *Early Mackinac.* The *New York Independent* called the volume "a delightful bit of romantic history," the *Detroit Free Press* thought it should "be regarded as historically exact in every detail" and the *Indianapolis Evening News* hailed it as "a model of restraint, condensation and accuracy." A second edition appeared in 1898 and sold for 50 cents in cloth and 25 cents in paper.

In the meantime, Williams continued his historical research. He visited libraries and wrote authorities such as Judge Joseph Steere of Sault Ste. Marie soliciting additional sources. New discoveries resulted in expanded editions of 163 pages in 1901 and 176 pages in 1903, published under the St. Louis imprint. Williams contemplated another larger book about the region, but it remained uncompleted at his death in 1906. His son, Jesse Lynch Williams, chose Duffield and Company of New York to publish a reprint of the 1903 revision with additional illustrations as *Early Mackinac: A Sketch Historical and Descriptive* in 1912.

Williams' labor of love, *Early Mackinac,* remains an excellent starting point for anyone who is captivated by the lure of the island and wants to learn more about its lore. His many excerpts from contemporary sources lend a fascinating reality to the book. Should readers, however, become interested enough to want to read more than the extracts provided by Williams they might encounter problems. Like many authors of his time Williams often failed to provide bibliographical information sufficient to permit identification of the original sources by other than an expert in the field. I have attempted to identify Williams major sources. In addition, without attempting comprehensiveness, I have unearthed additional works apparently unavailable to Williams, published subsequent to his death or not within his focus.

The first printed information about the Mackinac area was recorded by the French Jesuit fathers. From 1633 through 1673 yearly reports of missionary activity were sent in manuscript to Paris and printed in French by Cramoisy. Reuben Gold Thwaites edited the definitive edition, *The Jesuit Relations and Allied Documents*, in 73 volumes published in Cleveland, 1896-1901. Thwaites' monumental work included all official and unoffical reports from 1601-1791 in French, Latin, Italian and English texts.

In the *Relation* of 1642 Father Barthelemy Vimont first wrote of the exploits of his friend, Jean Nicolet,the coureur de bois who discovered the straits of Mackinac in 1634. Consul W. Butterfield authored the best scholarly account of the event, *History of the Discovery of the Northwest by John Nicolet* (Cincinnati: 1881). Father Jean Claude Allouez recorded the first account of Mackinac Island in the *Relation* of 1669. Other important references to the straits region occur throughout the *Jesuit Relations.*

In 1673, the Jesuit, Pere Jacques Marquette,departed from the missionary station he had founded at St. Ignace to explore the western country. His canoe voyage would take him to the Mississippi River. Marquette recorded his travels in *Voyages et Decouverts. ..de l'Amerique* (Paris: 1681). The great Catholic historian, John Gilmary Shea, first made available an English translation, *Discovery and Exploration of the Mississippi River* (N.Y.: 1852). Joseph P. Donnelly, a professor of History at Marquette University, published a scholarly biography, *Jacques Marquette, S.J.* in 1968.

Another Jesuit father whose name is immortalized on the Michigan map, Pierre Francois-Xavier Charlevoix, traveled from Detroit to Mackinac in 1721 and then down the east coast of Lake Michigan to the St. Joseph River. The erudite historian and traveler published his narrative in Paris in 1744. The first English translation appeared as *Journal of a Voyage to North America* (2 volumes, London: 1761).

A soldier, Baron Louis Armand de Lahontan, left his post near Detroit to explore the Mackinac region and the west in the 1680's. His account of the journey appeared as *New Voyages to North America* in 1703 in a French edition published at Hague and an English translation in London. Reuben Gold Thwaites edited a reprint of the English edition of 1703 published in Chicago in 1905.

The struggle for control of North America that had shed French and English blood since the early 1600's rocked the midwest in the mid 18th century. Charles de Langlade sallied forth from Michilimackinac to lead northern Indians against British settlements in the Ohio country. Publius V. Lawson's *Bravest of the Brave: Captain Charles de Langlade* (Menasha, Wisconsin: 1904) offers a detailed biography of this Mackinac born fur-trader and soldier.

Despite Langlade's efforts, New France fell to the British in 1760. The following year, the first British garrison occupied the fort at the present site of Mackinac City. Pontiac's Conspiracy soon broght renewed violence to the region. In 1763 Pontiac's braves gained entrance to the fort through the ruse of a ball game and massacred the entire garrison. Alexander Henry, a British fur trader, miraculously escaped the slaughter and wrote an exciting account of the battle and his subsequent hair breadth escapes. Henry did not publish his *Travels and Adventures* (N.Y.: 1809) until he was seventy, but it became a major source for many later authors including Francis Parkman. The first edition is rare and valuable. James Bain in 1901 and Milo Quaife in 1921 edited more easily accessible editions.

Following Pontiac's defeat, the British returned to Fort Michilimackinac in 1764. Two years later a remarkable new commandant arrived, Major Robert Rogers. A romantic hero of the French and Indian War and Pontiac's Conspiracy, Rogers could handle a pen as well as a hatchet and rifle. In 1765 he had published in London *A Concise Account of North America*, an accurate discussion of the American interior, including a description of Fort Michilimackinac, based largely on his personal knowledge. But Rogers' private affairs were not at par with his other achievements, and his fortunes ebbed and flowed. He remained at Fort Michilimackinac for 15 months until his arrest and trial for treason at Montreal. William L. Clements, the famous Michigan book collector, first published "Rogers Michilimackinac Journal" in the *Proceedings of the America Antiquarian Society*, Vol. 28, 1918.

While commandant at Michilimackinac, Rogers had sent a self-taught surveyor and map-maker, Jonathan Carver, on an expedition to discover a northwest passage to the Pacific. Carver related his experiences, including a description of the fort he had set out from, in *Travels Through the Interior Part of North America...1766-68* (London: 1778). Unfortunately Carver died in poverty in 1780, but his book became an influential best seller, going rapidly through 30 editions in six languages.

Williams' *Early Mackinac* skirts the period following the massacre to the removal of the fort to Mackinac Island, and for good reason. Little published information was available during his lifetime. Subsequently, however, a number of valuable records have come to light. In 1914 Clarence M. Burton presented to the Detroit Public Library the book and manuscripts concerning the history of Michigan he had been assembling for forty years. Among this collection were the papers of John Askin, a fur trader at Mackinac from 1767-1780, and in particular his letter book for 1778. Milo Quaife edited *The John Askin Papers* (Detroit: 1928) in two volumes. A decade later the Clements Library at the University of Michigan published *Old Fort Michilimackinac* with a foreword by Kenneth Roberts. This reproduction of two maps from the papers of General Thomas Gage contains an interesting letter from Captain

B. Glazier describing the fort in 1769. Another important source, acquired by Burton in 1914, first saw print in 1960 as *The Doctor's Secret Journal*. George May edited surgeon mate Daniel Morison's vivid account of rough and tumble life at the fort in 1769-1772.

The British abandoned Fort Michilimackinac in 1780 to build a more defensible fort on Mackinac Island. Following the Revolutionary War, the Treaty of 1783 ceded the island to the Americans, but it would not be until 1796 that the British finally evacuated Fort Mackinaw for St. Joseph Island. Eleven years later Canadian statesman George Heriot traveled through the straits. He penned a good description of the island and the fort in *Travels Through the Canadas* (London: 1807)

The Americans surrendered Fort Mackinaw to the British during the War of 1812 but won it back through the Treaty of Ghent in 1814. Soon the island became the capital of John Jacob Astor's American Fur Company, and a new era of bustling commercial activity followed. The advent of steam ships on the upper Great Lakes made travel easier, and increasing numbers of visitors found their way to Mackinac Island. By the 1820's, Mackinac served not only as a trading outpost but increasingly became a tourist mecca. Curious Americans, British and Canadians of diverse occupations arrived, and many published travel narratives recording information unavailable elsewhere.

John J. Bigsby, a British army surgeon and geologist, visited Mackinac Island in 1822 while serving as secretary to the British Boundary Commission that ran the line between Fort Williams and Lake of the Woods. The commission found, much to the chagrin of the soldiers who had relocated their fort on Drummond Island following the War of 1812, that their island lay on the American side. Bigsby published his narrative as *The Shoe and Canoe*...(2 vols, London: 1850), a rare volume.

Thomas L. McKenney, head of the newly created Office of Indian Affairs, stopped off at Mackinac Island while returning from negotiating a treaty at Fond du Lac in the summer of 1826. McKenney recorded in *Sketches of a Tour to the Lakes...* (Baltimore: 1827) a statement repeated by many later visitors, "Mackinaw is really worth seeing." The volume also contains one of the earliest lithograph views of the island.

Two other travelers recorded descriptions of the island in 1830. The Rev. Calvin Colton, journalist, politician and author, tarried there briefly while enroute from Detroit to Green Bay via steamer. Upon returning to England he wrote *Tour of the American Lakes...*(2 vols, London: 1833) Mrs. Juliette Kinzie, in company with her husband, Chicago pioneer John Kinzie, passed through on their way from Detroit to Chicago. She penned a good description of the island at the height of the fur trading era in *Wau Bun* (N.Y.: 1856).

The decade of the 1830's seems to have been a heyday for authors at Mackinac. Godfrey Vigne, an English barrister, wrote *Six Months in America* (2 vols, London: 1832). He stayed at the island in 1831 and amused himself by shooting great quantities of pigeons. An American doctor from New York, C.R. Gilman, arrived in October 1835 and visited with resident Indian agent Henry Schoolcraft. Back home the following year he published his account *Life on the Lakes...*, in two volumes. George W. Featherstonhaugh, a British geologist, also penned a description of the island in 1835 in *A Canoe Voyage up the Minnay Sotor* (2 vols, London: 1847).

A cultivated British authoress toured Michigan during the summer of 1836. Harriet Martineau described her trip overland from Detroit to Chicago and hence by steamer to Mackinac Island in *Society in America* (3 vols, London: 1837). Anna Jameson, an English writer and art critic, arrived the following summer. She recorded a good description of the island and a conversation with Schoolcraft in *Winter Studies and Summer Rambles in Canada* (3 vols, London: 1838). Captain Frederich Marryat, British author of popular sea and adventure tales, toured the island that same summer. His impressions survive in *A Diary in America...*(3 vols., London: 1839). Another British writer, soldier and sportsman, Captain R.G.A. Levinge, happened along in 1839 in time to see the colorful pageantry of the annual distribution of presents to the tribes. His recollections appeared in *Echoes From the Backwoods...*(2 vols., London: 1846).

An American authoress, Eliza Steele, chronicled her trip via steamer in 1840, which included a visit to the Schoolcraft family on the island, in *A Summer Journey in the West* (N.Y.: 1841). A woman of greater literary fame, Sarah Margaret Fuller (Ossoli), wrote a picturesque description of the island in *Summer On the Lakes, in 1843* (Boston: 1844). Two years later, James Beaven, an Anglican clergyman and Professor of Divinity in the University of King's College, Toronto, took a sabbatical to visit northern Indian missions. He recorded a lively description of the annual distribution of payment to the Ottawa at Mackinac Island in *Recreations of a Long Voyage...*(London: 1846).

The year, 1846, witnessed the arrival of at least three literary tourists. Paul Kane, a Canadian artist in search of Indian subjects, captured his experiences in *Wanderings of an Artist...*(London: 1859). Michigan's first native born professional author, Charles Lanman, provided an excellent description of Mackinac in *A Summer in the Wilderness* (N.Y.: 1847). Lanman's *Records of a Tourist* (Philadelphia: 1850) contains several legends he heard from an Ottawa while sitting on the brow of Arched Rock. William Cullen Bryant, America's earliest poet of distinction, stopped twice at the island in 1846. He wrote in *Letters of a Traveler...* (New York: 1850) that Mackinac could not escape its destiny of becoming a famous "watering place." Another professional American travel writer and lecturer, Bayard Taylor, left a description of the island in 1855 in *At Home and Abroad* (New York: 1860).

Some other visitors to the island buried descriptions in volumes with misleading titles. *Rustlings in the*

Rockies...(Chicago: 1883) by George O. Shields predominantly sketches of western hunting and fishing adventures, also includes a chapter, "The Island of Mackinac" describing a 1878 hunting expedition to northern Michigan. Similarly, appended to A. Judd Northrup's *Camps and Tramps in the Adirondacks* (Syracuse, N.Y.: 1880) is a narrative about a fishing trip to northern Michigan in 1879 featuring a voyage by excursion boat from Charlevoix to Mackinac Island.

Travelers continued to pen accounts of Mackinac in the twentieth century. In *Highway and Byways of the Great Lakes* (New York: 1911) Clifton Johnson recorded lengthy verbatim conversations with a local game warden and a 60 year native of the island who he met at the wharf. Lewis R. Freeman's *By Waterways to Gotham* (New York: 1926) describes his 2,000 mile voyage by motorboat from Milwaukee to New York City. Freeman took refuge from a sudden squall on Mackinac Island.

Autobiographies rank next to travel narratives as a primary source of Mackinac Island history. Henry Rowe Schoolcraft, who resided in the "Old Agency House" from 1833-1841, produced *Personal Memoirs of Thiry Years...*(Philadelphia: 1851), a fat volume crammed with details. *Incidents and Events in the Life of Gurdon S. Hubbard* (Chicago: 1888) provides an excellent description of the fort in 1818 and an eye witness account of the shooting of Alexis St. Martin. An unrelated namesake from Detroit, Bela Hubbard, described a geological expedition to the Upper Peninsula that departed from Mackinac Island in 1840 in *Memorials of a Half Century* (New York: 1887).

Missionary activity among the northern Indians produced other important records. John H. Pitezel, who spent nine years proselytizing in the Lake Superior country, wrote *Lights and Shadows of Missionary Life...* (Cincinnati: 1857). He described a visit to Mackinac Island in 1843 en route to missionary endeavors at the Sault, Ontonagon, etc. Fur trader Robert Stuart hired a young women from New York to tutor his five children in 1830. Eliza Chappell stayed several years and became active in Rev. William Ferry's United Foreign Missionary School. Excerpts from her Mackinac Island journal for 1832 appear in Mary H. Porter's *Eliza Chappell Porter: A Memoir* (Chicago: 1892). In 1831 the Massachussets Sabbath School Union published, in Boston, Sarah Tuttle's *Conversations on the Mackinaw and Green Bay Indian Missions.*

Before leaving the field of primary sources, that is, information recorded by actual witnesses, I want to mention some publications that contain both primary and secondary sources. The *Michigan Pioneer Collections* (40 vols., Lansing: 1877-1929) is an indispensable source for Mackinac history. The two volume index should be consulted for hundreds of references to primary documents and secondary histories of the region. Similarly, the index to the *Wisconsin Historical Collections* (20 vols., Madison: 1855-1911) contains nearly as many references. Of special note are Elizabeth Therese Baird's "Reminiscences of Early Days on Mackinac Island" in volume 14 and volumes 18-20 on the Mackinac Register and the fur trade.

The Michigan Historical Commission sponsored several publications relating to Mackinac history. Its Bulletin Number 5 contains Rev. Frank A. O'Brien's *Names of Places of Interest on Mackinac Island* (Lansing: 1911). Ida Amanda Johnson's *The Michigan Fur Trade* (Lansing: 1919) offers a scholarly study of the subject with much of Mackinac. The Commission's *Michigan History Magazine*, first published in 1917, contains many relevant articles such as Marion Morse Davis' *"Three Islands"* in volume 12. An index covering the issues from 1917-1962 is available.

Generations of historians have used the foregoing primary sources to delineate the history of the Mackinac region. Mormom leader Jesse James Strang published the first such history at the Beaver Island Print Shop in 1854. It was reprinted in 1885, 1894 and 1959. While tinged by Strang's own opinions, it is basically a reliable history. William Peter Strickland consulted many earlier accounts and interviewed long time residents to produce the first substantial history, his 404 page *Old Mackinaw or the Fortress of the Lakes and Its Surroundings* (Philadelphia: 1860).

The island's colorful past and romantic surroundings, in conjunction with long winter evenings, stimulated a number of residents to try their hand at history. Reverend J.A. Van Fleet became the first to practice a tradition later followed by Meade Williams. He resided in the Old Agency Building while preparing *Old and New Mackinac* (Ann Arbor: 1870). Van Fleet's well researched volume had gone through three editions by 1880.

A soldier stationed at the fort, Lt. Dwight H. Kelton, devoted the "long dreary evenings of the Mackinac winter" to research in old records at the fort, American Fur Company papers and village and county records. His resulting publication, *Annals of Fort Mackinac* (Chicago: 1882) was hawked on steamers to the island and had gone through 13 editions by 1895. Kelton's history was superceeded that year by Lt. Col. John Read Bailey's *Mackinac Formerly Michilimackinac* (Lansing: 1895). Bailey had led a distinguished army medical career. He became attending surgeon at the fort in 1854, served in the Civil War and returned as U.S. physician for the Ottawa and Chippewa Indians at Michilimackinac. By the 1890's he also operated the National Park Drug Store where copies of his 220 page publication could be procured at 25¢ paperbound. By the time of the volume's 5th revision in 1904, Bailey had become a commissioner of the Mackinac Island State Park.

Stanley Newton, a newspaperman from Sault Ste. Marie, wrote a 187 page volume *Mackinac Island and Sault Ste Marie* (Sault Ste Marie: 1909). Two decades later, Roger Andrew, another newspaperman and a Mackinac Island Park Commissioner, produced *Old Fort Mackinac: On the Hill of History* (Menominee: 1938). Bay City resident, Raymond McCoy, turned out another popular account of the region and a paraphrase of Alexander Henry's narrative *The Massacre of Old Fort Mackinac* (Bay City: 1950).

Edwin O. Wood, a past president of the Michigan Historical Commission and Mackinac Island Park Commissioner, wrote the most significant history of the area. The two large volumes of *Historic Mackinac* (New York: 1918) are virtually an encyclopedia of the history of Mackinac Island and vicinty. A comprehensive bibliography adds to the work's usefulness.

Other histories have appeared in more recent years. The completion of the Mackinac Bridge inspired William Ratigan to write *Straits of Mackinac* (Grand Rapids: 1957), a collection of historial episodes told in a popular vein. Veteran historian Walter Havighurst turned out a readable military history of the region, *Three Flags at the Straits* (Englewood Cliffs, N.J.: 1966) for Stewart Holbrook's American Forts Series. And most recently, Russell McKee edited *Mackinac the Gathering Place* (Lansing: 1981) an excellent book replete with color and stereo illustrations.

County and regional histories also contain information relevant to the region of the straits. George Robinson and R.A. Sprague produced the first slim county history, *History of Cheboygan and Mackinac Counties* (Detroit: 1873). A decade later, A.T. Andreas edited the massive *History of the Upper Peninsula of Michigan* (Chicago: 1883). It includes 191 pages on the general history of the region and 28 pages on Mackinac County. Alvah L. Sawyer's *History of the Northern Peninsula*...(3 vols., Chicago: 1911) and George N. Fuller's *A History of the Upper Peninsula* (vol 3 of *Historic Michigan*...Dayton: 1926) offer additional biographical information.

John B. Mansfield's *History of the Great Lakes* (2 vols., Chicago: 1899), a compendium of great lakes history and commerce, contains much on Mackinac including New York politician Thurlow Weed's narrative of his 1847 trip by steamer to Mackinac Island. Other useful volumes about the great lakes include Harlan Hatcher's *The Great Lakes* (New York: 1944); Fred Landon's *Lake Huron* (Indianapolis: 1944); Milo Quaife's *Lake Michigan* (Indianapolis: 1944) and Walter Havighurst's *The Great Lakes Reader* (Toronto: 1969).

Histories not oriented to a narrow geographic focus also contain vital information. Renowned American historian Francis Parkman's works, *History of the Conspiracy of Pontiac* (Boston: 1851) and *France and England in North America* (9 vols., Boston: 1865-92) have yet to be bettered. *The History of the Ottawa and Chippewa Indians of Michigan* (Ypsilanti: 1887) by Andrew J. Blackbird presents two chapters on Mackinac history from the Indian point of view. Famed Wisconsin historian Reuben Gold Thwaites' *How George Rogers Clark Won the Northwest* (Chicago: 1903) includes "The Story of Mackinac." Calvin Goodrich wrote a valuable chapter on Michilimackinac in *The First Michigan Frontier* (Ann Arbor: 1940). Sara A. Shafer contributed a chapter on Mackinac to *Historic Towns of the Western States* (New York: 1901) edited by Lyman P. Powell. And an interesting chapter on "Fort Michilimackinac and Fort Holmes" appears in John Martin Hammond's *Quaint and Historic Forts of North America* (Philadelphia: 1915).

Archaeological explorations at Mackinac have uncovered new information and resulted in a body of literature. The Michigan State University dig during the 1959 season is the subject of a 130 page volume, *Excavation at Fort Mackinac...*(East Lansing: 1961) by Moreau S. Maxwell and Lewis Binford. Dirk Gringhuis wrote and illustrated a juvenile book, *The Big Dig: A Frontier Fort Comes to Life* (New York: 1962) about the same excavation. Eugene Petersen has contributed *Michilimackinac Its History and Restoration* (Fort Mackinac: 1962) and *Gentleman on the Frontier...*(Mackinac Park Commission: 1964).

Ephemeral publications such as guide books, promotional brochures, souvenir pamphlets and transportation schedules, normally are soon discarded. If they survive they may become prime historical sources. John Disturnell's *A Trip Through the Lakes of North America...*(New York: 1857) was one of the first travel guides to the upper Great Lakes and further popularized northern tours. It contains descriptions of the region, recommended routes and sailing schedules. Disturnell also produced the first guide book to the island,*Island of Mackinac...*(Philadelphia: 1875) with a folding hand-colored map. Other guide books representative of the genre include: Foster and Reynold's *The Standard Guide, Mackinac Island and Northern Lake Resorts* (n.p.: 1899 & 1904); James Gale Inglis' *Northern Michigan...*(Petoskey: 1898) and Florence Fuller's *Map and Guide of Mackinac Island* (n.p.: 1926).

Transportation lines put out promotional publications, heavy with hyperbole but often lavishly illustrated with valuable photographs. The Michigan Central Railroad sponsored Patrick Donan's *Mackinac Island: The Wave-Washed Tourist's Paradise of the Unsalted Seas* (St. Louis: 1882) and Frank J. Bramhall's *In Summer Days* (Chicago: 1886). The Detroit and Cleveland Steam Navigation Company tried to stimulate trade with Helen K. Ingram's *Three on a Tour* (Detroit: 1895). Other rare illustrations have been preserved in published souvenir pamphlets including: Adolph Witteman's accordion folded lithographic views *Mackinac Island* (New York: 1886); E.J. MacAdam's *Picturesque Mackinac* (Brooklyn: ca 1890), in photogravure; B.F. Childs' *Marquette, Mackinac Island and the "Soo"* (N.Y.: 1889); W.H. Gardiner's *Ancient and Picturesque Mackinac* (Grand Rapids: 1905); E.W. Wallace's *Pictorial Mackinac Island* (Mackinac Island: 1907) and numerous series of post card folders from the 1920's - 1940's.

The plethora of travel narratives, autobiographies, histories and other books about the island, to say nothing of its uniquely picturesque qualities, induced many fictional writers to take pen in hand. One of America's earliest successful authors, Washington Irving, pioneered the field with *Astoria* (New York: 1836), a novel about John Jacob Astor's fur empire set in part on Mackinac Island. Three-quarters of a century would pass before another male novelist chose the island as a setting. William Levere wrote *Vivian of Mackinac* in 1911. Harold Titus, a talented writer from Traverse City, followed Irving's theme in *Black Feather* (Philadelphia: 1936). Titus later wrote that he conceived his plot "alone one moonlit summer night looking up at the chaste facade of the old John Jacob Astor House at Mackinac Island."

Kenneth Roberts' *Northwest Passage* (New York: 1937) celebrated the life of Robert Rogers and became a best seller. *River and Empty Sea* (Boston: 1950), Louis Vaczck's tale of Jesuits and the fur trade, was set in part in 17th century St. Ignace. David Garth wrote *Fire on the Wind* (New York: 1951), a popular novel about Upper Peninsula lumbering set in part on Mackinac Island. Myron C. Orr completed a trilogy about the Mackinac fur trade, *Citadel of the Lakes* (New York: 1952), *Mission to Mackinac* (New York: 1956) and *The Outlander* (New York: 1959).

The major body of Mackinac fiction, however, has flowed from pens held by feminine hands. Constance Fenimore Woolson earned a degree of fame as an early realist beginning with her collection of short stories, *Castle Nowhere: Lake-Country Sketches* (Boston: 1875). Two of the stories had Mackinac Island settings. A granddaughter of James Fenimore Cooper, Woolson spent several summers at Mackinac as a girl. The plot of her first novel, *Anne* (New York: 1882),was a Mackinac Island romance. A biography, *Constance Fenimore Woolson* (London: n.d.) by Clare Benedict includes additional short stories and poetry about Mackinac.

Another popular author of regional fiction during the 1890's, Mary Hartwell Catherwood, chose Mackinac Island as a setting. The *White Islander* (New York: 1893) is a novel about Alexander Henry, Wawatam and the massacre at Fort Michilimackinac. Her collection of short stories, *Mackinac and Lake Stories* (New York: 1899) contains pieces set on Mackinac Island and Round Island. Julia Altrochi wrote one of the best Michigan novels, *Wolves Against the Moon* (New York: 1940) about the life of Mackinac fur trader Joseph Bailey. Iola Fuller also published *Loon Feather*, a novel about the fur trading era, in 1940 and won the prestigious Hopwood Award.

In addition to these successful novels, Mackinac Island inspired a good number of pot-boilers. Cynthia Gorton's *Fatal Secret*...(Philadelphia: 1873) was based on the life of Rev. Chauncey Hall who operated a missionary school on the island. Mrs. Mary Virginia (Hawes) Terhune's *With Best Intentions* (Chicago: 1890); Anna Johnson's *An Abundant Harvest* (Cincinnati: 1904); Alice P. Smith's *Montlivet* (Boston: 1906) and Mrs. Edna W.S. Troops' *Blackbird, A Story of Mackinac Island* (Detroit: 1907) are sacharine love stories.

Other fictional writers set out to captivate a juvenile audience. Joseph E. Badger dashed off a dime novel *Caribou Zip; or, the Forest Brothers, a Tale of the Fall of Michilimackinac* (New York: 1874). E.A. Allen's *A Jolly Trip*...(ca 1890) is a story about a voyage to Mackinac Island on the "City of Alpena" and a stay at the Grand Hotel. Margaret Frances Fox wrote *Betty of Old Mackinaw* (Boston: 1901) for the "Cozy Corner Series." Louis Arundel's *Motor Boat Boys on the Great Lakes or Exploring the Mystic Isle of Mackinac* (Chicago: 1912) went through several editions. *Sandy MacDonald's Man* (Lansing: 1929) by Richard C. Ford is about the Mackinac fur trade. Mabel Leigh Hunt set her handsome volume, *Michel's Island* (New York: 1940), in the days of the voyageurs.

The Poetic Muse also frequently moved Mackinac visitors to rhapsody. Captain Thomas Morris came to America with the British Army in 1758 and was stationed for some time at Michilimackinac. In 1791, he published, in London, *Miscellanies in Prose and Verse*, much of which had been composed at the fort. Col. Arent Schuyler De Peyster served as commandant at Michilimackinac from 1774-79 and while there wrote a variety of poetry about local scenes, incidents, Indians, etc. Following the war he settled down in Dumfries, Scotland where he developed a friendship with the local excise man and companion poet, Robert Burns. Burns addressed one of his last pieces, written in 1796, "Poem on Life," to his friend Col. De Peyster. In 1813 De Peyster published in Dumfries his own poetry, *Miscellanies by an Officer*.

Periodically, other poetic effusions, invariably published via the vanity press, made their appearance. Angie Bingham Gilbert presented a tiny six page offering *Devil's Kitchen, Mackinaw Island* (Grand Rapids: 1886). Joseph Frazier, a soldier stationed at the island, produced a more substantial assemblage, *Sunset at Mackinac and Other Poems* (Sault Ste Marie: 1893). Lorena Maybelle Page converted Indian tales into poetry in *Legendary Lore of Mackinac* (Cleveland: 1901). Warren W. Lamport, a Methodist minister from Benton Harbor with a flair for rhyme, wrote a number of poems dealing with the region of the straits. "Skilligalee" and "Mackinac" were often reprinted.

Now, I could venture into the area of literary references to Mackinac such as are found in Herman Melville's *Moby Dick* and Edward Everett Hale's *The Man Without a Country*, but I fear I have already taxed your patience with juvenile literature and poetry. Let me close by urging you to start with Meade C. Williams, and read him carefully. Then, if the literature of Mackinac intrigues you, this essay should help you find additional volumes.

Larry B. Massie

Allegan, Michigan

EARLY MACKINAC

CHAPTER I

Michilimackinac was the old-time name, not for our beautiful island alone, but for all the country round about us, north to Lake Superior and west to the head of Green Bay. It was the island only that was first thus called. The word grew out of it, and small bit of land though it is, it threw its name over a vast territory.

The name has been variously spelled. In old histories, reports, and other documents, I have found Mishlimakina, Missilimakinac, Mishilmaki, Michilimachina, Michilimaqina, Missilimakina, Michiliakimawk; while in one standard history, when this region is spoken of, it invariably appears as Michilimakinaw.[1] In its abbreviated form it has been written Mackinack, Macina, Maquina, Mackana, Mackinac, Mackinaw. In all the earlier periods following the settlement of the island by the whites, in books of travel and of history, and in mercantile records, *Mackinac* and *Mackinaw* were used interchangeably, though the form Mackin*aw* was most commonly adopted. Also in many of the early maps and atlases it is also given. Steamboat companies doing business on the island generally advertised their boats

[1] Henry Adams' "*History of the United States.*"

as of the " Mackinaw Line. Business firms so wrote the word — at least as frequently as the other form. So this was quite general during all that time, except that the official name of the military post held to the termination " ac." But since the railroad companies built their modern terminal town across the straits and called it Mackinaw City, for the sake of convenience in distinguishing, the name of the island is now uniformly written Mackinac. In pronunciation, however, without attempting to settle the question by the laws of orthoepy, it may be remarked that it is considered very incorrect to sound the final *c;* and that to the ears of residents, and old *habitues* and lovers of the island, it is almost distressful and irritating to hear it called anything other than Mack-in*aw*. The pronunciation which has prevailed in the locality and throughout the surrounding region for generations past has become the law of usage, and should determine the question. It is said that among the early residents of the island there was but one person who ever called it Mackina*ck*, and he was regarded, in his day, " as an eccentric." A compromise may perhaps be allowed, by taking the name as if it bore the termination *ah,* and giving it a sound between the flat and the very broad. Julian Ralph, a noted American traveler and descriptive writer, has referred to the subject, and says the confusion is due to the French manner of " gallicizing " the words of any language they touch, so that all through our West, where they had early settlements, they thus " spelled words one way and pronounced them another, in a style peculiar to their own language, and maddening to the blunt and practical Anglo-Saxon mind." And he charges us to remember that the name is always Mackin*aw,* no matter how it is spelled. Another traveler visiting the island in 1830, and writing about it, after first giving its name in full as Michilimackinack, says that in conformity with popular usage, "we will henceforth say "*Mackinaw.*" Col. Wm. M. Ferry, of Park City, Utah, who lived on the island as a boy from 1824 to 1834, and who has a wide intelligence concerning its early local history, tells me the Canadian Frenchmen sounded it as Mack-ee-naw, and from that it came into common use. The word is further familiar to us from what, in our summer wear, is called the "Mackinaw hat." And the "Mackinaw boat," as descriptive of a certain build of sailing craft common long ago in these straits, is a term still written as of yore.

The origin and signification of the word is in some obscurity. All agree that the first part of it, "Michi," means great. It is preserved in the name of the state, Michigan, and in the name of the lake, Lake Michigan — meaning great waters. The French took it up, spelling it Missi; hence the name of the river Mississippi — great river, the father of waters. Concerning the remainder of the name which follows Michi, we are not so sure. The common view is that the form of the island, high-backed in the center, as it rises above the waters, and handsomely crowning the whole, suggested to the Indian fancy the figure of a turtle. Hence that it became known as the land of the Great Turtle.

Heriot, an English traveler in North America, who published his "Travels through the Canadas" in 1807, touched at Mackinac and reports as the origin of the name that the island had been given, as their special abode, to an order of spirits called Imakinakos, and that "from these aerial possessors it had received the appellation of Michilimackinac."

Schoolcraft, who is the best authority on all questions pertaining to the Indian language, as well as to the customs and characteristics of that race, says that the original name of the island was Mishi-min-auk-in-ong, and that it means the place of the great dancing spirits — these spirits being of the more inferior and diminutive order, instead of belonging to the Indian collection of gods; a kind of pukwees, or fairies, or sprites, rather than Manitous.

At the time of his first visit to the island in 1820, Schoolcraft was inclined to the common view which connected the name with the turtle. But later, after he had lived many years among the Indians, and had made a study of their language and their modes of thought, he preferred the other explanation. The transition from the Indian Mishi-min-auk-in-ong to the French Michilimackinac he thus explains: The French used *ch* for *sh,* interchanged *n* for *l,* and modified the syllables *auk* and *ong* respectively into *ack.* Perhaps the *ack,* or *ac* as we now have it, is but a suggestion of the nasal sound they would give to the final syllable *ong,* in the Indian word. A further hint may be furnished in the fact that the French form of the name, as we find it in old historical records and other documents, so frequently bears the termination *ina* instead of *ack.* We have, then, only to give the broad sound to the final *a,* to see how Mackin*aw* may have become a common pronunciation. A philological explanation, strictly scientific, is not claimed. Many local words, especially geographical terms, throughout all the upper lake regions of early settlement, show corruptions as they have passed from the Indian language first into the French of the early explorers and missionaries, then into the *patois* of the illiterate French Canadians, and then into a mongrel anglicized form.[1]

Perhaps the different views as to the signification of the word — the great turtle, or the great spirits — can in a manner be combined. The turtle was held in great reverence by the Indians. In their mythology it was regarded as a symbol of the earth and addressed as mother.[2] The fancied physical resemblance of the island could easily work in with their mythical idea of the turtle, apart from its

[1] *Bois Blanc,* the French name of the large island near Mackinac became *Bob b'low,* and then in popular speech drifted into *Bob-i-low.* Near the head of Lake Michigan, is a small island (now a light-house spot), named by the French *Ile aux Galets,* but which in local phraseology has become *Skilli-ga-lee.* And north of it, at the entrance to the Straits, and also marked by a light-house, is *Wau-go-chance,* which is often designated colloquially as Wau-go-shanks, sometimes as "Wabble-shanks," and by some of the steamboat men, consulting brevity, "The Shanks."

[2] Andrew Lang, in his "*Myths, Ritual and Religious*" (vol. 1, p. 182), mentions certain of the Indian tribes as holding the fancy that the earth grew out of the tortoise. One form that the legend took was that Atahenstic, a woman of the upper world, had been banished from the sky, and falling, dropped on the back of a turtle in the midst of the waters. The turtle consulted with the other aquatic animals and one of them, generally said to have been the musk-rat, fished up some soil, and fashioned the earth. Here the woman gave birth to twins and thus began the peopling of the globe. Thus in the crude fancy of the Western Indians do we find a reflection or fragment of the ancient myth which once prevailed in the oriental mind that the world rested on the back of a turtle.

having any etymological connection. And thus whatever way the name is studied it becomes associated with some Indian conception of spirit. All singular or striking formations in the work of nature — objects that were of an unusual kind, or very large and imposing, as lofty rocks, overhanging cliffs, mountains, lakes and such like — these poor untutored

OTTAWA CANOE.

children looked upon as the habitations of spirits. Our island, therefore, physically so different from the other islands and the mainland about it, with its glens and crags, and its many remarkable and strange-looking stone formations, would easily be peopled for them with spectres and spirits. They regarded it as their sacred island — a sort of shrine — and a favorite haunt of their gods, and cherished for it feelings akin to awe; and from the surrounding regions would bring their dead for burial in its soil. It seems to have been rather their place of resort and temporary sojourn than of permanent abode.

There is something very fascinating in the fragments of early Indian fancies and traditions and legends which are associated with our island. It is interesting, too, to note how the legends and the mythology of the Indians and their dim religious ideas so often took a poetic form. For instance, in their pagan and untutored minds they thought of the island as the favorite visiting place of Michibou, the great one of the waters, their Manitou of these lakes. That coming over the waters from the sunrise in the east, he would touch the beach at the foot of Arch Rock; that the large mass of stone which had fallen from the face of the cliff in the long ago, causing the arch above, was "Manitou's Landing Place"; that the arch was his gateway through which, ascending the hill, he would proceed with stately step to "Sugar Loaf," which in fancy they made to be his wigwam, or lodge — the cave on the west side, known to all to-day, being his doorway. Then again, the Sugar Loaf Stone and others of that conical, pyramidal shape — such as the one which stands in St. Ignace, and those in different parts of the northern peninsula, and yet others which formerly stood on this island — that these strange, uncanny-looking rock formations, by a modification of fancy, they would personify into great giants or monsters who towered over them as sentinels to note whether they made due offerings and sacrifices to Manitou, their success in hunting and trapping being conditioned on this kind of religious fidelity.[1]

The Indians, so spontaneously recognizing the world of spirits, were fruitful in ideas and sentiments of reverence. We are told there were no profane words in their vocabulary. Think of a people who did not know how to swear because they had no words for it. It is said that the nearest they approached to cursing a man was to call him " a bad dog." [2] So, too, in the nomenclature of wild, uncouth-looking objects of nature. While our white pioneers and prospecting miners and *avant couriers* of civilization in the West have so often attached to such objects the name of the devil, as " Devil's Lake," " Devil's Slide," " Devil's Half-acre," " Devil's Scuttle-hole," and such like, the Indians generally gave

[1] Schoolcraft noted a curious fact among the Chippewas — that they fancied the woods and shores and islands were inhabited by innumerable spirits who during the summer season were wakeful and quick to hear everything that was spoken, but during the winter existed only in a torpid state. The Indian story tellers and legend mongers were therefore very free in amusing their listeners with fanciful and mysterious tales during the winter, as the spirits were then in a state of inactivity and could not hear. But their story telling was suspended the moment the piping of the frog announced that spring had opened. That he had endeavored, but in vain, to get any of them to relate this sort of imaginary lore at any other time than in the winter. They would always evade his attempts by some easy or indifferent remark.

[2] " I have made many inquiries into the state of their vocabulary, and do not, as yet, find any word which is more bitter or reproachful than *matchi annemoash,* which indicates simply bad dog. They have terms to indicate cheat, liar, thief, murderer, coward, fool, lazy man, drunkard, babbler. But I have never heard of an imprecation or oath. The genius of the language does not seem to favor the formation of terms to be used in oaths or profanity. It is the result of the observation of others as well as my own, to say, that an Indian cannot curse." Schoolcraft's " *Thirty Years with the Indian Tribes.*"

them some expressive and harmonious poetic name. On the island we have the "Devil's Kitchen," but we may feel sure that was not of the Indian's naming. The writer of this sketch learned from an old resident who had passed the whole of an extremely long life on the island, that once, long ago, a shoemaker took up his abode in that cavern and did his cobbling and his *cooking* there. Possibly that gave rise to the name.

In this habit of nomenclature which linked their ideas with the phenomena of physical nature, we see a beautiful though often rude and childish vein of poetry. Their name for the great cataract of Niagara was "Thunder of the Waters," as that for the gentle falls now within the limits of the city of Minneapolis, was Minnehaha or "Laughing Waters." The familiar white fish of these regions was the "Deer of the Waters." To the horizon limit, when they looked out on the lake to where the thread-like line of blue water loses itself in the clouds and sky, they gave the name which signified the "Far-off Sight of Water." The name for General Wayne, who did so much to overthrow their power in the West, was "Strong Wind"; while the American soldiers, from their use of the sabre and sword in battle, were known as the "Long Knives." Their conception of a fort, with its mounted cannon, was "The high-fenced house of thunder," while the discharge was, "The arrow that flies out of the big gun." Their word to designate the Christian Sabbath, meant "Prayer Day." The month of February they called "The moon of crusted snow," as the snow could then bear up a man in the hunt, while the feet of the stag would break through. In the personal names given to individuals we often see a poetic association with the objects of nature most familiar to their minds. A little son of Mr. Schoolcraft, then government agent at the Sault, was admiringly called by the Chippewas "Penaci," or "The Bird;" while the name of Mrs. Schoolcraft's mother, a full-blooded Indian woman, was a many-syllabled word, which meant "Woman of the Green Valley." The English authoress, Mrs. Jameson, when visiting the Sault, after "shooting the rapids" with the Indian guides (the first European woman who had ever ventured on the exploit) was re-named "The Woman of the Bright Foam." I find the names of five Indian chiefs, each as translated giving quite a poetic sense: The Sun's Course in a Cloudless Sky, Bursts of Thunder at a Distance, The Sound of Waves Breaking on the Rocks, The Returning Clouds, The Bird in Eternal Flight.[1]

As their whole life and range of observation was constantly associated with tempests, forests, waters, skies, and all the various phenomena of physical nature, this gave shape to their conceptions and their questionings. It has always seemed very significant that when John Eliot, the pioneer missionary to the Indians in New England two hundred and fifty years ago, began his instructions among them, he was met at once by their eager and long pent-up questions of wonder: "What makes the sea ebb and flow?"

[1] In contrast, we note in their modern reservation and semi-civilized life a degeneracy in the style of names they are fond of bearing, such as Sitting Bull, Thunder Bull, Crazy Snake, Wolf-in-the-middle, Ground Nose, Creeping Bear, Man-afraid-of-his-horses, Rain-in-the-face, etc.

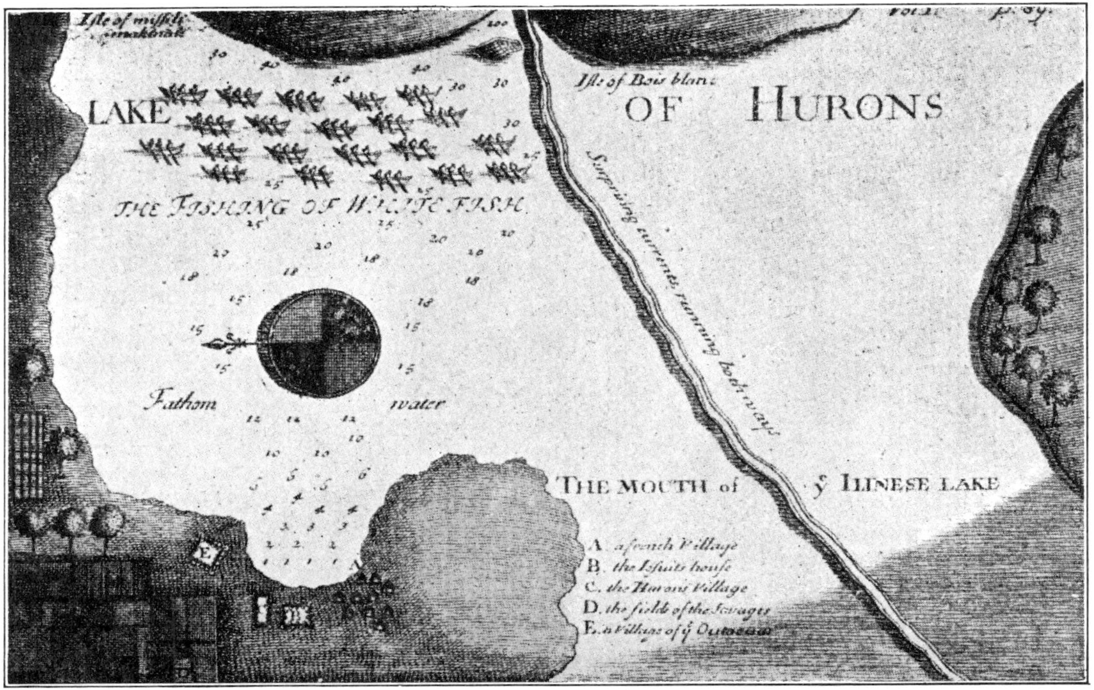

LA HONTAN'S SKETCH — 1688.

Islands Mackinac, Round, and Bois Blanc at top of Picture. Northern Peninsula of Michigan and Point St. Ignace in fore-ground. Southern Peninsula on the right. The Early French by "Ilinese Lake" meant Lake Michigan.

"What makes the wind blow?" "What makes the thunder?"

Parkman represents the Jesuit missionaries in Canada, two centuries since, as testifying that the Indians had a more acute intellect than the peasantry in France. At his best, however, the red man was but the "child of the forest," and in the presence of the pale faces was not destined to endure. They are a doomed and a passing race —"meeting the fate they cannot shun." Many reasons or causes might be assigned for this. One reason is that which was given by a very thoughtful Indian in a speech on a certain occasion long ago, before a company of government agents here on the island beach. Said he, very reflectively: "The white man no sooner came than he thought of preparing the way for his posterity; the red man never thought of that." In this profound observation is embodied one of the latest deductions in social philosophy.

Of course, in thus speaking of the Indians, reference is had to manifestations of their mental character as seen in the earlier days, and not to Indian life and character at present, as seen in the Western reservations. By contact with the whites, it has been said, they lost their originality.[1]

[1] Catlin, who ranks next to Schoolcraft in his study of the Indians, in an extensive classification of qualities, contrasts their original character in their "primitive and disabused state," with their secondary character after "being beaten into a sort of civilization." From being handsome, he says, they had become ugly; from free, enslaved; from affable, reserved; from bold, timid; from warlike, peaceable; from proud, humble; from independent, dependent; from healthy, sickly; from sober, drunken; from increasing, decreasing; from landholders, beggars."

"In their own woods they are a noble race; brought near to us, a degraded and stupid race."—Mrs. Jameson.

"The imprisoned lion in the showman's cage differs not more widely from the lord of the desert, than the beggarly frequenter of frontier garrisons and dram-shops differs from the proud denizens of the woods. It is in his native wilds alone that the Indian must be seen and studied."—Parkman in "*History of the Conspiracy of Pontiac.*"

CHAPTER II

The annals of our island since its discovery and occupation by the whites carry us back to an early day. Explorers from France and settlers from Canada were here two hundred and fifty years ago. Traces of French and Indian mixture are everywhere seen. Indian wars and massacres have reddened these shores. Stories of English power victorious over French, in far back colonial times, have a part in the history of this region. In a later day the island had its stirring incidents in our own war with Great Britain, in 1812. Here was the headquarters of the Mackinaw Fur Company and the Southwest Fur Company, and afterwards of the powerful American Fur Company, of which John Jacob Astor was the chief proprietor, and which made our island for the time the largest seat of commerce in the western country.[1] Christianity, too, has had here its early enterprises, at the hands first of the French Jesuit missionaries of the 17th Century, and afterwards of Protestantism.

In regard to early military annals, history points to the fact that with the exception of the brief abandonment by the French forces from about 1701 to 1714, this region of the straits had been a seat of con-

[1] Detroit, Vincennes, St. Louis, Lake Winnipeg, Lake of the Woods, and other far distant points were but dependencies of Michilimackinac, as the metropolis of the Indian trade.

tinuous military occupation from the last quarter of the 17th Century down to 1895, when to the surprise and regret of all who knew the island's history, the United States Government abolished the post. Three different flags have floated over a fort in these Straits of Mackinaw during this long period past. These have been in the order of French, English and American. The French were the pioneers. They established Fort Michilimackinac, over where now the town of St. Ignace stands, four miles across on the northern peninsula. This was about two hundred and twenty-five years ago.

Baron La Hontan, who had come from France to Canada at an early age and afterwards became Lord Lieutenant of a French Colony in Newfoundland, visited our Mackinac neighborhood in 1688. In a publication of his travels in North America he gives three letters from the Michilimakinac settlement of that day.[1] As accompanying his picture on the adjoining page he thus writes: "You can scarce believe what vast sholes of white fish are catched about the middle of the channel, between the continent and the isle of Missilimakinac. The *Outaouas*[2] and the *Hurons* could never subsist here, without that fishery; for they are obliged to travel about twenty leagues in the woods before they can kill any harts or elks, and it would be an infinite fatigue to carry their carcasses so far over land. This sort of white fish, in my opinion, is the only one in all these lakes that can be called good; and indeed it goes beyond all

[1] The book was first published in French, 1705. Afterwards an enlarged edition appeared in English form, 1735.

[2] Ottawas.

other sorts of river fish. Above all, it has one singular property, namely, that all sorts of sauces spoil it, so that it is always eat either boiled or broiled, without any manner of seasoning.

"In the channel I now speak of, the currents are so strong that they sometimes suck in the nets, though they are two or three leagues off. In some seasons it so falls out that the currents run three days eastward, two days to the west, one to the south, and four northward; sometimes more and sometimes less. The cause of this diversity of currents could never be fathomed, for in a calm they will run, in the space of one day, to all the points of the compass, *i. e.,* sometimes in one way, sometimes another, without any limitation of time; so that the decision of the matter must be left to the disciple of Copernicus.

"Here the savage catch trouts as big as one's thigh; with a sort of fishing-hook made in the form of an awl, and made fast to a piece of brass wire, which is joined to the line that reaches to the bottom of the lake. This sort of fishery is carried on not only with hooks, but with nets, and that in winter as well as in summer.

"The *Outaouas* and the *Hurons* have very pleasant fields, in which they sow Indian corn, pease and beans, besides a sort of citruls and melons. Sometimes these savages sell their corn very dear, especially when the beaver hunting happens not to take well; upon which occasion they make sufficient reprisals upon us for the extravagant price of our commodities."

For a short interval the French Government, under the instigation of the post Commander, Cadillac, withdrew the garrison (as already mentioned) and abandoned this region as a military seat in favor of the new settlement at Detroit. That was about the opening of the 18th century. But this vacating was soon seen to be bad policy, and in 1714 the fort was re-established. When, however, the restored fort becomes known again in history, it is found located on the Southern Peninsula, across the Straits, where now stands the railroad town, Mackinaw City. Whether on the return from Detroit the military at once located the fort there, or first resumed the old site at St. Ignace, and removed to the other Peninsula at some later period, is not definitely known. At any rate it was the same military occupation, and the same Fort Michilimackinac, irrespective of the time of change in the site. It stood about half a mile from the present Light House, and southwesterly from the railroad station; and was so close to the water's edge that when the wind was in the west the waves would often break into the stockade. Its site is plainly visible to-day, and visitors still find relics in the sand.

After the conquest of Canada by the English, in the deciding battle of Quebec on the heights of Abraham in 1759, all this country around came under the English flag. The Indians, however, liked better the French dominion and their personal relations with the French people than they did the English sway and English associations, and they did not take kindly to the transfer. One reason for this preference is said to have been that the French were accustomed to pay respect to all the Indians' religious or superstitious observances, whereas an Englishman or an American

OLD FORT MICHILIMACKINAC ON SOUTH SIDE OF THE STRAITS.

Taken from sketch made in 1820 and published in Schoolcraft's "Ethnological Researches among the Red Men," issued by act of Congress. Alexander Henry, who dwelt for a time at this fort, says it covered about two acres of ground; that the settlement consisted of traders and their families (French Canadian) along with the English soldiers; that about thirty houses, including a French Church, and all that made up the life of the community, were comprised within the stockade.

was apt, either to take no pains to conceal his contempt for their superstitions or to speak out bluntly against them. To this can be added the well known fact of the greater readiness of the French to intermarry and domesticate with the Indian.[1]

This strong feeling of discontent under the change of empire, on the part of the Indians, was fanned and skillfully directed by that great leader and diplomate, Pontiac;[2] and "The Conspiracy of Pontiac" is the well-known title of one of Parkman's series of North American history. This conspiracy was no less than a deep and comprehensive scheme, matured by this most crafty savage chief, for a general Indian rising, in which all English forts, from the south to the upper lakes, were to be attacked simultaneously, and the English rule forever destroyed. The Indians would vauntingly say, "You have conquered the French, but you have not conquered us." Out of twelve forts, nine were taken, but not long held.

While this scheme was, of course, a failure in its larger features, the plot against the old post of Michilimackinac across the water succeeded only too well. The strategy and horrors of that capture read like a

[1] "When the French arrived at this place," said a Chippewa Chief at a council once held at the Sault, "they came and kissed us. They called us children and we found them fathers. We lived like brothers in the same lodge."—*Schoolcraft, in an address before the Michigan Historical Society in* 1830.

[2] "In force of character, subtlety, eloquence and daring, Pontiac was perhaps the most brilliant man the Indians of North America have produced."—"*A History of Canada,*" by Chas. G. D. Roberts. Schoolcraft rated him in the same way. Drake, in his "*Indians of the Northwest,*" says of him: "His fame in his time was not confined to his own continent but the gazettes of Europe spread it also."

tale of fiction. The story is old, but to repeat it in this sketch will not be amiss. It may be introduced under the title of

AN HISTORIC BALL GAME.

In 1763 a band of thirty-five English soldiers and their officers formed its garrison. Encamped in the woods not far off was a large number of Indians. One morning in the month of June, with great show of friendliness, the Indians invited the soldiers to witness their match game of ball, just outside the stockade. The Chippewas were to play the Sacs.[1] Then, as now, ball playing had great fascination. And as this was the birthday of the King of England, and the men were in the celebrating mood, some indulgence was shown, discipline for a time relaxed, gates were left ajar and the soldiers and officers carelessly sauntered and looked on, enjoying the sport. In the course of play, and as a part of the pre-concerted stratagem, the ball was so struck that it fell within the stockade line of the fort. As if pursuing it, the players came rushing to the gate. The soldiers, intent in watching the play, suspected nothing. The Indians now had an open way within, and instantly turned from ball-players into warriors, and a terrifying "whoop" was given. The squaws, as sharing in the plot, were standing near with tomahawks concealed under their blankets. These were seized, and then followed a most shocking massacre. The surprise of the fort and the success of the red men were complete.

[1] Baggatiway was their kind of ball game.

The details of this dreadful event are vividly and harrowingly given by the English trader, Alexander Henry, sojourning at the time, with his goods within the stockade, and unfortunately a sharer in the dreadful scenes and experiences. The humble Henry may well be called the Father of History, like another Herodotus, as far as this episode is concerned. Excepting the very meagre report of the humiliating capture made by Captain Etherington, the officer in command, there seems to be nothing but the narrative of this English trader. His description of the fort, the purpose it had been serving, the movements of the Indians preceding the affair, as well as the minute description of the stratagem and its success, and the terrible scenes enacted, is the chief source of information; and one can take up no history of this period and this locality without seeing how all writers are indebted to his plain and simple narrative.

When the fort was captured by the savages, he himself was hidden for the first night out of their murderous reach, but was discovered the next day. Then followed a series of experiences and hair-breadth escapes and turns of fortune very remarkable, while all the time the most barbarous fate seemed impending, the suspense in which made his sensations, if possible, only the more distressful and torturing. It was not enough that his goods were confiscated and his very clothes stripped off his body, but his savage captors thirsted for his blood. They said of him and their other prisoners, that they were being reserved to "make English broth." After four days of such horrors there came a turn which Henry says gave "a new color to my lot." During his residence at the post before the massacre, a certain Chippewa Indian named Wawatam, who used to come frequently to his house, had become very friendly and told him that the Great Spirit pointed him out as one to adopt as a brother, and to regard as one of his own family. Suddenly, on the fourth day of his captivity, Wawatam appeared on the scene. Before a council of chiefs he asked the release of his brother, the trader, at the same time laying down presents to buy off whatever claims any may have thought they had on the prisoner. Wawatam's request, or demand was granted, and taking Mr. Henry by the hand he led him to his own lodge, where he received the utmost kindness.

A day or two afterwards, fearing an attack of retaliation by the English, the whole body of Indians moved from the fort over to our island as a place of greater safety. They landed, three hundred and fifty fighting men. Wawatam was among them, with Henry in safe keeping. Several days had passed, when two large canoes from Montreal, with English goods aboard, were seized by the Indians. The invoice of goods contained among other things, a large stock of liquor, and soon mad drunkenness prevailed. The watchful and faithful Wawatam told Henry he feared he could not protect him when the Indians were in liquor, and besides, as he frankly confessed, "he could not himself resist the temptation of joining his comrades in the debauch." He therefore took him up the hill and back in the woods, and hid him in a cave, where he was to remain hidden "until the liquor should be drank." After an uncomfortable and unrestful night, Henry discovered next morning, to his horror, that he had been lying on a heap of human bones and skulls. This charnel-house retreat is now the well-known "Skull Cave" of the Island, one of the regular stopping places of the tourists' carriages.

ALEXANDER HENRY.

But we cannot follow trader Henry's fortunes farther. In a relation between guest and prisoner, and generally treated with respect, moving with the band from one place to another, following the occupation of a hunter, and taking up with Indian life and almost fascinated by it, he at length finds himself at the Sault, where soon an opportunity opened for his deliverance and his return home. Subsequently he made another trip to the country of the upper lakes and remained for a longer time. Of his good friend Wawatam, it is a sad tradition that he afterwards became blind and was accidentally burned in his lodge on the island at the Point, formerly known as Ottawa Point, in the village, then as Biddle's, and more recently as Anthony's Point.

It may be that some have felt incredulous in respect to Henry's thrilling tale. But there is reason to think it entirely trustworthy. It is contained in a book which he wrote, entitled "Travels and Adventures in Canada and the Indian Territories, between 1760 and 1776." It was first published in 1809, and is dedicated to Sir Joseph Banks, "Baronet of His Majesty's Privy Council and President of the Royal Society." It is a book of thrilling interest. It has long been out of print, and copies of it to-day are very rare and command a high price. Mr. Henry's residence in his latter years was at Montreal, and he was still living as late as 1811, an old man past eighty years of age, hale and cheerful looking. He bore a good name and an unquestioned reputation for veracity among those who knew him. I have already named him the Herodotus of this particular period of history. By another person, an enthusiastic English visitor at Mackinac, over sixty years ago, he was called also the Ulysses of these parts; and of his book it was said it bore the relation to the Michilimackinac shores and waters which the Odyssey does to the shores of Sicily.[1]

[1] The chronological order in which early travelers and visitors, who have left any annals of their journeys, came to this

region, may be stated as follows: Niccollet, in 1634; Marquette, 1671; LaSalle and Hennepin, 1679; LaHontan, 1688; Charlevoix, 1721; Alexander Henry, 1762; Capt. John Carver, 1766.

CHAPTER III

The victory of the Indians over at the old fort on the Southern mainland was nothing beyond a shocking and atrocious massacre. It was utterly barren as regards any permanent results, and the status of supremacy was not changed. The stockade had not been destroyed, and British troops soon came and resumed possession. Subsequently, however, the question of transferring the military seat of the Michilimackinac region across the Straits to our island came up, and was duly considered. Major Sinclair made a careful preliminary examination. In a letter written in October, 1799, he says: "I employed three days from sun to sun in examining the Island of Mackinac, on which I found great quantities of excellent oak, elm, beech and maple, with a vein of the largest and finest cedar trees I ever saw. . . . The soil is exceedingly fine, with abundance of limestone. . . . The situation is respectable, and convenient for a fort." He also mentions that he found on the island "a run of water, sufficient for a saw mill."

He submitted drawings and cuts of the island, and plans for fortification, to Gen. Haldimand, the officer in command of the department, and whose headquarters were at Quebec. The superiority of the island, as a strong position against Indian attacks, and Indian threats and insults, was pointed out; also its advantages in having one of the best harbors in the upper country, and as respects the fishing interests likewise. It is thought, too, that the transfer was somewhat connected, in the British mind, with the American war of the Revolution, which was then in progress. Sinclair spoke of the "liability of being attacked by the Rebels," at the old fort, and that the place might "justly be looked upon as the object of a separate expedition." As a precautionary measure, he made every trader take oath of allegiance to the king, and to hold in "detestation and abhorrence the present unnatural and horrid rebellion." At any rate, the garrison did not feel safe in a mere stockade of timbers on the mainland. Gen. Haldimand accordingly gave orders for the removal. The following letter on the subject was written by him, April 16, 1780, to Major DePeyster, formerly in command of the old Mackinac fort, but who had been transferred, the year before, to the command at Detroit.[1]

"Sir — Having long thought it would be expedient to remove the fort, etc., from its present situation to the Island of Michilimackinac, and being encouraged in this undertaking by advantages enumerated by Lt. Gov. Sinclair, that must result from it, and the earnest desire of the traders, I have given directions that necessary preparations, by collecting ma-

[1] Major DePeyster was of American birth, and had served in the British army in various parts of this country, besides commanding at Mackinac, and afterwards at Detroit. He held a commission for 77 years, and lived to the age of 96. He spent his latter years in Dumfries, Scotland, the early home of his wife. During his residence there, he and the poet Burns were great friends. Burns addressed one of his fugitive poems to DePeyster.

terials, etc., be made with as much expedition as possible, as the strength of that post will admit of. I am sure it is unnecessary to recommend to you to furnish him every assistance he may require, and that Detroit can afford, in forwarding this work, farther than by giving you my sanction for the same, which I do in the fullest manner."

A government house and a few other buildings were at once erected on the site of the present village; the old block houses were built, and His Majesty's troops took possession on the 13th of July, 1780, Major Sinclair commanding, though the entire removal was only gradually effected.

The Indians, as proprietors of the land, had been first consulted about this occupancy, and agreement and treaty terms were obtained. The consideration was £5,000. Two deeds were signed, with their mark, by four chiefs, in behalf of themselves and all the Chippewas. One was to be lodged with the Governor of Canada, and one to remain at the island post; while the chiefs engaged to preserve in their villages a belt of wampum seven feet long, to be a memorial of the transaction. But it seems that after the work was under way and the post established, the Indians showed discontent, and threatened the troops; and so serious was the hostility manifested, that Sinclair sent in great haste to Detroit for cannon. The vessel was back in eight days, bringing the guns, and as soon as she touched on the harbor she fired a salute, and that "speaking out" by the cannon's mouth at once settled the question, and the poor Indians had no more to say.

The old site being abandoned (since when it is

often referred to as "Old Mackinaw,") and the garrison removed, the families of the little settlement, could not do otherwise than follow the fort. Many of the houses were taken down and transported piecemeal across the straits, and set up again as new homes on the island. And hardly were the settlers thus re-established before they addressed a petition to the government, asking for remuneration to compensate for the loss and expense incurred, on the ground that their removal was in the interest of the State and the public welfare. What response was made to this petition I have found no record which tells.

The first commandant of the island, Major Sinclair, was also known as Lieutenant Governor. It appears that he had been appointed inspector and superintendent of the English forts, and bore some general civic position as representative of the government, besides his military rank; also as having charge of Indian affairs. Hence he is frequently spoken of in the records as Gov. Sinclair, as well as Major. It seems to have been on this account, as an officer with a more embracing scope, rather than as of higher military rank, that he superseded Major DePeyster, in command at old Mackinac, in 1779. After the transfer he remained two years in charge of the new post. Sinclair appears, from the style of his letters and reports, a more cultured and better educated man than some of his cotemporaries among the officers of that period. But his services as a post commandant and general manager of affairs, seem to have been unsatisfactory, because of his lavish expenditures, and because of "abuses and neglects in different shapes," as it was said. He was continually being cautioned from headquarters in regard to his financial transactions. For half a century and more, after he left the post, the inhabitants continued to talk about his extravagance; and one of the stories long current on the island, was that he had paid at the rate of one dollar per stump for clearing a cedar swamp in the government fields at the west end of the village. It subsequently appears that, on his return to England, this recklessness in expenditure while on the island led to his imprisonment for debt. He speaks himself, in one of his letters, of being "liberated upon paying the Michilimakinac bills protested."

Major, or Governor, Sinclair was succeeded by Captain Daniel Robertson, who seems to have been in command from 1782 to 1787. This Robertson is also called Robinson, and is the one whose name will probably be always associated with the island, and a figure mark in the guide books and the traditionary stories — for when will "Robinson's Folly" cease to be visited and talked about?

The official annals of that time show a great many of Captain Robinson's letters, written while he was commandant of the post. He seems to have been a rough-and-ready, energetic officer; not very elegant in his style of composition or his orthography, prosaic and practical, and perhaps not quite fulfilling the sentimental and romantic ideal which some of the legends and stories, connecting his name with the "Folly," would suggest. In one of his reports of this time, a very good plat is given, showing the contour of the island and the location of the fort, and the harbor bearing the name, "Haldimand's Bay," named, presumably, in honor of the English commander of the province.[1] In a letter of April, 1783, the Captain commends the climate of Mackinac as "preferable to any in Canada, and very healthy;" but he says "it is an expensive place." He tells in 1784 of the wharf being broken to pieces by the ice, so that no kind of craft could be loaded or unloaded, but that he set men to work and got it in repair. He adds: "It was a very troublesome job." He wants to know, he says, in one of his letters, whether or not he is to "have any rum;" and again he says, he is at a loss to know how he is to act at this post without that liquor, and he is sorry he is "obliged to cringe and borrow rum from traders on account of Government." At another time he writes, "I have had no rum this season, and you know it is the Indian's God." And yet again he pours forth his complaint: "Rum is very much wanted here for various purposes, particularly for Indians, and I have had only seven barrels this twelve month."

However, it is but due to the Captain to say that, unfortunately, he was not alone in this opinion of the indispensableness of rum in the relations of the whites and the military with the Indians. We find Major Sinclair, his predecessor, as commandant of the fort, writing to General Haldimand in 1781, as follows: "The Indians cannot be deprived of nearly their usual quantity of rum, however destructive it is, without creating much discontent." There is a sad vein running through all this early history, made

[1] The name was evidently given up after the island changed its flag. In the early days, subsequent, it was familiarly designated by the island people as "The Basin."

by rum; first as one of the government supplies to the Indians, and next as an article of traffic. The poor red men facetiously called it "The English Milk;" but their more serious name for it was the truer one, "Fire water."[1]

Robertson (Robinson) was in command from 1782 to 1787. There are intimations of his having been disapproved at Gen. Haldimand's headquarters, and we are told that during those days of British occupancy, just as in the administration of affairs since that time in our own western outposts, "abuses in the Indian department were common." Captain Scott was next put in command, "sent in the room of Robertson," as the record reads. This change seems to have been for the great improvement of the service. An officer sent out from Montreal, on an inspection tour, thus reports concerning Scott: "I do not believe there is a better man in the world, or a more zealous good officer of his standing in the army. He has gained infinite credit during his command at Mackinac, but, poor fellow, his pocket has paid for it. Yet he has convinced the people there that it is possible for a commanding officer to be an honest and an honorable man. He will tell you wonderful stories of the Indian department in

[1] H. M. Robinson in his interesting book, "The Great Fur Land," descriptive of the regions of the Hudson's Bay Company, says of the Indian's liquor, "It must be strong enough to be inflammable, for he always tests it by pouring a few drops in the fire."

"The effects of ardent spirits in the lodge, are equal to the appearance of a grizzly bear amongst them."—*Schoolcraft.*

"An Indian would barter away all his furs, nay even leave himself without a rag to cover his nakedness, in exchange for that vile unwholesome stuff called English brandy."—Willson's, "*The Great Company.*"

FORT MACKINAC TO-DAY.

that quarter." Scott was followed in command of the post by Captain Doyle, who remained in charge until its delivery to the United States.

The fort was not built complete at once, but gradually took on its dimensions and its strength. In 1789, after an inspection by the Engineer's Department, the fortifications, as originally designed, were reported as being only in part executed, and that the work had been discontinued for some years, and that in the mean time a strong picketing had been erected around the unfinished works. And again, as late as 1792, the plans were reported as not yet finished; the officers' stone quarters were only about half completed; the walls were up the full height and the window frames in, but the roof and floors wanting. (Sharp criticism was made, too, by the officer then inspecting, on the whole design of the fort.) And yet again, in 1793, the commandant, Captain Doyle, writes concerning the "ruinous state of the fort," but says he purposed "sending to the saw mill for planks, and would give the Barracks a thorough repair, having received orders from His Excellency, Maj. Gen. Clarke, to that purpose;" also asking for "an engineer and some artificers to render the miserable fortress in some degree tenable."

Even after its transference to the United States it was only by slow degrees brought on to its better condition as a fortification. Heriot in his visit to the island in 1807 (already referred to) reports the fort as "consisting of four wooden block-houses, . . . the space between being filled up with wooden pickets." Again, in 1817, Samuel A. Storrow, who had been a judge advocate in the army, visiting Mackinac, describes the fort as "a platform enclosed with palisades." He mentions, as did Heriot, four block-houses. It was the same rude and primitive style of fortification when first seen by Schoolcraft in 1820. It was still, however, in the early period of the century that the fort took on its present features. Its lines have been somewhat changed and much of

VIEW FROM THE FORT.

the stone work has been built since the British founded it in 1780. The block-houses now standing are the originals; and within the memory of all but a very few of the oldest inhabitants there have been but the three we now see. The fourth one was near the southeast corner, perhaps on the spot of the old gun-platform on which for so many years stood the two cannon which used to give the morning and evening salute in the days when the fort grounds were a garrison post. Another and much steeper path than the present one then led up the hillside. There was a very good well within the inclosure. This well and also a Powder Magazine were near the east Sally-Port and the present Quartermaster's building.

In its inception and planting it is a military structure of a century ago, and with scarcely a feature to make it a fort of to-day's construction. It is a memento of the past and is replete in historic reminiscence. As a fortification, it is a curious mixture of American frontier post and old-world castle. Its thick walls and sally-ports, and bastions and ditch, its old block-houses of logs, loop-holed for musketry, its sloping path down to the village street buttressed along the hillside with heavy masonry, above which grow grass and cedars up to the foot of the overlooking old "officer's quarters"— all this makes it a striking and picturesque object, a sort of mountain fortress, and certainly something unique in this country.

CHAPTER IV

The war of the revolution had been fought and American independence acknowledged. But although the treaty of Paris in 1783 had secured all this upper lake country on the same general boundary lines as they run to-day, and Great Britain had stipulated that her troops should withdraw with all convenient speed, yet it was thirteen years afterward before the island came under our jurisdiction, and before the nation's flag floated over the fort. It was the same in respect to four or five other military posts situated on the American side of the lakes. Washington, at the time President of the United States, had promptly sent Baron Steuben to Montreal to receive the forts from General Haldimand according to the treaty stipulations, but Haldimand replied he had no instructions from his government to make the delivery, and that he could not even discuss the subject. General Knox was sent on the same errand in 1784 and likewise Col. Hull, but without accomplishing the object. The Government, by John Adams, our minister to England, insisted on the same, but to no effect.

Great Britain urged in explanation of her refusal the imperfect fulfillment on the American side of certain of the treaty stipulations. Some of the States of the Union had passed resolutions staying proceedings at law for all debts due to English creditors; and some had taken action relative to those citizens who during the struggle had adhered to the mother country, and who had been known as Tories — action which was regarded by Great Britain as contrary to the treaty. Such grounds were made the plea for retaining these border posts. Our government responded that Congress had done all that lay within its power when it earnestly recommended to the States concerned, the repeal of all enactments which might conflict with the requirements of the treaty.[1]

It was understood that Great Britain was loth to surrender this territory which, by reason of the extensive fur trade it afforded, was sure to become of great commercial importance. It is probable, too, a lingering belief that the experimental young Republic was not destined to a long career, and that there might soon come opportunity of renewing English dominion, made an element in the policy of delay.

Negotiations were pending for a long time, and it required another treaty (this question however being only one of the many points embraced) before the tardy transfer of these posts was effected. It was called the "Treaty of Amity, Commerce and Navigation" and was secured under the hand of the American plenipotentiary, John Jay. By that treaty, it was stipulated that on June 1st, 1796, the forts should be evacuated by the British and turned over to the United States. Owing to delays on the part of Congress, our occupation of the posts was deferred beyond that date. As Washington said in his address to Congress, December, 1796:

[1] Whitelock's Life of Jay. Life and works of John Adams, vol. 8, p. 355.

"The period during the late session, at which the appropriation was past for carrying into effect the treaty of amity, commerce and navigation, between the United States and His Britannic Majesty, necessarily procrastinated the reception of the posts stipulated to be delivered, beyond the date assigned for that event." He adds: "As soon, however, as the Governor General of Canada could be addressed with propriety on the subject, arrangements were cordially and promptly concluded for their evacuation, and the United States took possession of them, comprehending Oswego, Niagara, Detroit, Michilimackinac and Ft. Miami." [1]

All the others of these frontier posts were delivered over at, or near, the date prescribed — in the months of June and July. But in the case of Fort Mackinac, it was not until October 2nd of that year that the actual transfer was made. This date shows that the last act in the war of the American revolution, and the final scene and seal of its triumph, is connected with our Island.[2]

But, besides negotiating with the English in the recovery of Mackinac, the American government had to deal with another class of proprietors — the original possessors of the soil. Accordingly, while the delivery of the island and post was still pending, Gen. Wayne's treaty with the Indians (Treaty of Greenville), was made in August, 1795, by which "a tract

[1] American State Papers.

[2] The Tablet, which the City of Detroit, Mich., at its Centennial celebration a few years since placed in the wall of the Government building, commemorating the delivery of the fort at that place, July 11, 1796, and which describes the evacuation as the "closing act of the war of independence," needs some modification.

of land was ceded on the main, to the north of the island on which the post of Michilimackinac stands, to measure six miles on Lakes Huron and Michigan, and to extend three miles back from the waters of the lake on the strait." [1] Bois Blanc, or White Wood Island, was also ceded as the voluntary gift of the Chippewas. The Indians were to receive $8,000 annually, besides $20,000 then distributed.

Perhaps the unfinished state of the post, as reported in 1792, and the complaint made of its condition in 1793, and its sore need of repairs (referred to above), may be explained on the ground that the English authorities, well knowing it was within American lines, and apprehending that it must soon pass out of their control, deemed it unwise to incur any large expenditure on it. In fact, we find Captain Robertson saying in a letter, as early as 1784, that in compliance with orders he had received, no more labor was given to a post which by treaty had been ceded to the Americans, than was necessary to "command some respect for the safety of the garrison and traders, surrounded as I am by a great number of Indians not in the best humor." It is probable, therefore, that when at length it came into our hands it was in need of considerable attention, for we find Washington, in the same address to Congress just quoted from, saying of these posts that "such repairs and additions had been ordered as appeared indispensable." [2] It is also probable that the American force sent to occupy the post at the departure of the British soldiers was quite imposing, as we have Tim-

[1] Holmes' *American Annals*, vol. 2, p. 402.
[2] American State Papers.

othy Pickering, Washington's Secretary of War, in his report of February, 1796, saying: "To appear respectable in the eyes of our British neighbors, the force with which we take possession of these posts should not be materially less than that with which they now occupy them. This measure," he adds, "is also important in relation to the Indians, on whom first impressions may have very beneficial effects."[1] Accordingly, the first detachment to occupy Mackinac, as an American garrison, consisted of four officers, one company of Artillery and Engineers, and one company of Infantry, Major Henry Burback being in command of the whole force. The British retired to the island of St. Joseph, on the Canada side a little above Detour, and established a fort there.

Following the change of flag and sovereignty, nothing very stirring seems to have developed in the island history during the years immediately succeeding. It soon became, however, a great commercial seat and emporium in the wilderness. The chief commodity was furs. From an early day this had been a business carried on by the individual traders who went among the Indians. In course of time these operations assumed a larger and more systematic form under the hands of strong chartered companies. Of this I shall speak later. The situation of the island in the far northern country, its direct communication by the great lakes with the remotest parts east, south, west and north, and its being the principal seat of white habitation and commerce and military authority on the watery highway,

MACKINAC BEACH (EAST END). SKETCHED IN 1843.

and the key to the whole upper country — all this gave it an extended reputation in that early day. Travellers, sometimes from Europe as well as from our own eastern states, would touch at the island, visit its fort and explore its woods and its natural curiosities even as is done now. The fur trade, together with other lines of traffic which it stimulated, made the island for many years a great commercial seat. It is reported, for instance, for the year 1804, that the goods entered at the Mackinac Custom House yielded a revenue to the United States of about $60,000.

While at this time our island was United States territory, and the fort with its ever floating flag was a visible token of its Americanism, the village as a whole, with its Indian and French population and its style of construction — much of its architecture being a kind of cross between the white settler's hut and the Indian's birch bark lodge — perhaps did not appear so characteristically American. Let us look at its picture as drawn by Washington Irving in his "Astoria." It is Mackinac as seen in 1810. He is describing an expedition under way for the far northwest and the head waters of the Missouri, in the interest of Mr. Astor's enterprises. The party had fitted out in Montreal, under Wilson P. Hunt, of New Jersey; and in one of the large canoes, thirty or forty feet long, universally used in those days in the schemes of commerce, had slowly made their way up the Ottawa river, and by the old route of the fur traders along a succession of small lakes and rivers, to our island. Here the party remained about three weeks, having stopped for the purpose of taking on more goods and to engage more recruits. Irving thus describes the place:

"It was not until the 22d of July that they arrived at Mackinaw, situated on the island of the same name, at the confluence of Lakes Huron and Michigan. This famous old French trading post continued to be a rallying point for a multifarious and motley population. The inhabitants were amphibious in their habits, most of them being or having been *voyageurs* or canoe-men. It was the great place of arrival and departure of the southwest fur trade. Here the Mackinaw Company had established its principal post, from whence it communicated with the interior and with Montreal. Hence its various traders and trappers set out for their respective destinations about Lake Superior and its tributary waters, or for the Mississippi, the Arkansas, the Missouri, and the other regions of the west. Here, after the absence of a year or more, they returned with their peltries, and settled their accounts; the furs rendered in by them being transmitted, in canoes, from hence to Montreal. Mackinaw was, therefore, for a great part of the year, very scantily peopled; but at certain seasons, the traders arrived from all points, with their crews of *voyageurs,* and the place swarmed like a hive.

"Mackinaw, at that time, was a mere village, stretching along a small bay, with a fine broad beach in front of its principal row of houses, and dominated by the old fort, which crowned an impending height. The beach was a kind of public promenade, where were displayed all the vagaries of a seaport on the arrival of a fleet from a long cruise. Here *voyageurs* frolicked away their wages, fiddling and dancing in the booths and cabins, buying all kinds of knick-knacks, dressing themselves out finely, and parading up and down, like arrant braggarts and coxcombs. Sometimes they met with rival coxcombs in the young Indians from the opposite shore, who would appear on the beach, painted and decorated in fantastic style, and would saunter up and down, to be gazed at and admired, perfectly satisfied that they eclipsed their pale-faced competitors.

"Now and then a chance party of 'Northwesters' appeared at Mackinaw from the rendezvous at Fort William. These held themselves up as the chivalry of the fur trade. They were men of iron, proof against cold weather, hard fare, and perils of all kinds. Some would wear the northwest button, and a formidable dirk, and assume something of a military air. They generally wore feathers in their hats, and affected the 'brave.' '*Je suis un homme du nord!*'—'I am a man of the north,' one of these swelling fellows would exclaim, sticking his arms akimbo and ruffling by the Southwesters, whom he regarded with great contempt, as men softened by mild climates and the luxurious fare of bread and bacon, and whom he stigmatized with the vain-glorious name of 'pork-eaters.' . . . The little cabarets and sutlers' shops along the bay resounded with the scraping of fiddles, with snatches of old French songs, with Indian whoops and yells."

But the reader must not think there was no other side to the social life of the early Mackinac of that period. Irving's picture is only that of the wharves, and the floating population, such as the manager of a water expedition, stopping over but a little while, would be the most likely to see. Although the resident population was very small, there were, at the same time, the families of settled homes, and with the social interests and sympathies and pleasures common to American village life — subject of course to many inconveniences and privations incident to their remoteness in a wilderness world. I find a pleasing description written by a lady, who was taken to the island when a child, in the year 1812, just before the war opened, and who spent the years of her girlhood there.

The houses of the village at that time, she says, were few, quaint and old. Every house had its garden enclosed with cedar pickets. These were kept whitewashed, as also the dwellings and the fort. There were but two streets in the village. One ran from point to point of the crescent harbor, and as near the water's edge as the beach would permit — the pebbles forming a border between the water and the road. (It will be remembered that the water's edge in earlier years was considerably more inland than now.) A foot path in the middle was all that was needed, as there were no vehicles of any description, except dog-trains or sleds in the winter. There were no schools, no physician, and no resident minister of religion.[1] Occasionally a priest would come on visitation to the Catholic flock. In winter the isolation was complete. Navigation closed usually by the middle of October, and about eight months were passed in seclusion from the outer world. The

[1] Schoolcraft at the time of his first visit to the island, in 1820, remarked on its need of a preacher, a school-master, an attorney, and a physician. "Of merchants," he adds, "there are always too many."

A VIEW OF EARLY MACKINAC.

Taken from sketch made in 1820 and published in Schoolcraft's "Ethnological Researches Among the Red Men," issued by act of Congress. The view is taken from Round Island. The defect in perspective is noticeable, but the picture is interesting by reason of its antiquity as well as for its substantial correctness.

mail came once a month "when it did not miss." There were no amusements other than parties. The children, however, made houses in the snow drifts, and coasted down hill. Spring always came late, and as it was the custom to observe May day they often planted the May pole on the ice. Once she records, for the 8th of May, "Ice in the Basin good." She relates that in the autumn of 1823 the ice formed very early, but owing to high winds and a strong current it would break up over and over, and be tossed to and fro, until it was piled to a great height in clear, towering blue masses; and all that met the eye across to the opposite island were beautiful mountains of ice. The soldiers and fishermen cut a road through. This made a winter's highway for the dog sleds, the passage winding between high walls of ice, with nothing to be seen but the sky above. Again, in other seasons, the ice would be perfectly smooth. The exciting times on the island, she says, were when *La Caneau du Nord* came. As the canoes neared the town there would come floating on the air the far-famed Canadian boat song. The *voyageurs* landing, the Indians would soon follow and the little island seemed to overflow with human life. These exciting times would last for six or eight weeks. "Then would follow the quiet, uneventful, and to some, dreary days, yet to most, days that passed happily." [1]

[1] Mrs. H. S. Baird, whose reminiscences of Mackinac were published in a Green Bay newspaper, 1882. They are preserved in the "Wisconsin Historical Collections," vol. 9. Mr. Gurdon Hubbard, identified with the business of the island in those early days, and acquainted with all its families, says of this lady, in his autobiography (1802–1886) that she was "highly educated and was considered the belle of Mackinaw."

It is interesting to find the following comment on Mackinac written by a visitor in the early period now spoken of, and to note his warm appreciation of the island then, and his prediction concerning its future: "Mackinaw is really worth seeing. I think it by no means improbable that it will become a place of fashionable resort for the summer. There is no

INDIAN WIGWAM.

finer summer climate in the world. The purest, sweetest air, lake scenery in all its aged and grand magnificence and the purest water. . . . No flies and no mosquitoes, nothing to annoy, but every variety for the eyes, the taste and the imagination." [1]

[1] Col. McKenney in 1826 — joint Commissioner with Governor Cass in negotiating with the Indians.

CHAPTER V

The year 1812 brought our second war with the mother country. In it our little island played a part, and indeed it may be said to have "opened the ball." The very first scene of the war was enacted here. The two governments had been under strained relations for some time before, and on the 19th of June, of that year, the state of war was declared by President Madison. It was a mystery at the time, and something which excited clamor and, in the frenzy of the hour, even insinuations of treachery against high officials at Washington, that the English commanders in Canada knew the fact so much in advance of our own. One explanation is that our very deliberate Secretary of War trusted to the ordinary postal medium in communicating with the frontier troops, while the agents of the English government sent the news by special messengers. General Hull, commander of the department of Michigan, said he did not receive information of the fact until fourteen days after war was declared; while General Brock, the British commander opposite, had official knowledge of it four or five days sooner. And likewise Lieutenant Hanks, of our island post, was in blissful ignorance of the fact, until he saw the British cannon planted in his rear, just four weeks after war had been determined upon.

The English officer, Captain Roberts, commanding

at the Island of St. Joseph, on the near-by Canada border, had received orders immediately to undertake the capture of the strategic point of Mackinac. He gathered a force, consisting of Canadian militia (the English Fur Co.'s *voyageurs* and other employees), and a large number of Indians, besides having the regular soldiers of the garrison. The expedition was admirably managed. An open attack in front would

WALK-IN-THE-WATER.

(FROM AN OLD TIME WOOD CUT)

First Steamboat on the Upper Lakes. Built in 1818. At Mackinac, June, 1819. Wrecked near Buffalo, Nov., 1821. Described by one of that day as "A weak but elegant boat."

have been impossible of success. So, secretly sailing from St. Joseph, they landed, unperceived, on the northwest side of the island, at 3 o'clock in the morning, on the spot known ever since as "British Landing." The troops had an unobstructed march across the island and were soon in position with their cannon on the higher ground commanding the fort in the rear, the Indian allies establishing themselves in the woods on either flank.

The American commandant and his little handful of men then learned, at the same moment, the two facts, that the United States and Great Britain were at war, and that the surrender of Fort Mackinac was demanded. Resistance was impossible, and thus again the flag was raised over its walls that had first floated there. Pothier, an agent of the Northwest Fur Company, who accompanied the expedition and commanded a part of the force, thus laconically reported it to Sir Geo. Prevort: "The Indian traders arrived at St. Joseph with a number of their men, so that we were now enabled to form a force of about two hundred and thirty Canadians and three hundred and twenty Indians, exclusive of the garrison. With that force we left St. Joseph on the 16th, at eleven o'clock A. M., landing at Michilimackinac at three o'clock the next morning, summoned the garrison to surrender at nine o'clock, and marched in at eleven"— just twenty-four hours after setting forth on their hostile errand. He adds further, that there were between two and three hundred other Indian warriors who had expected to join the expedition, but failed; that two days after the capitulation, they came. But he intimates that this band was in an undecided state of mind and partly inclined to favor the Americans.

Captain Roberts, in his report to General Brock, dated the day of the capture (July 17th), says: "We embarked with two of the six pounders and every man I could muster, and at ten o'clock we were under weigh. Arrived at three o'clock A. M. One of those unwieldy guns was brought up with much difficulty to the heights above the fort and in readiness to open about ten o'clock, at which time a summons was sent in and a capitulation soon after agreed on. I took immediate possession of the fort and displayed the British colors."

As presenting an American account of the surprise and capture, the official report of Lieut. Hanks is herewith given. It was made to Gen. Hull, his commanding officer, and was issued from Detroit, whither the officers and men of the captured garrison had been sent on parole:

"DETROIT, August 12th, 1812.

"SIR — I take the earliest opportunity to acquaint Your Excellency of the surrender of the garrison of Michilimackinac, under my command, to His Britannic Majesty's forces, under the command of Captain Charles Roberts, on the 17th ultimo, the particulars of which are as follows: On the 16th, I was informed by the Indian interpreter that he had discovered from an Indian, that the several nations of Indians then at St. Joseph (a British garrison, distant about forty miles) intended to make an immediate attack on Michilimackinac. . . .

"I immediately called a meeting of the American gentlemen at that time on the island, in which it was thought proper to dispatch a confidential person to St. Joseph, to watch the motions of the Indians.

"Captain Michael Dousman, of the militia, was thought the most suitable for this service. He embarked about sunset, and met the British forces within ten or fifteen miles of the island, by whom he was made prisoner and put on his parole of honor.

He was landed on the island at daybreak, with positive directions to give me no intelligence whatever. He was also instructed to take the inhabitants of the village, indiscriminately, to a place on the west side of the island, where their persons and property should be protected by a British guard, but should they go to the fort, they would be subject to a general massacre by the savages, which would be inevitable if the garrison fired a gun. This information I received from Dr. Day,[1] who was passing through the village when every person was flying for refuge to the enemy. I immediately, upon being informed of the approach of the enemy, placed ammunition, etc., in the block houses; ordered every gun charged, and made every preparation for action. About nine o'clock I could discover that the enemy were in possession of the heights that commanded the fort, and one piece of their artillery directed to the most defenseless part of the garrison. The Indians at this time were to be seen in great numbers in the edge of the woods.

"At half past eleven o'clock the enemy sent in a flag of truce demanding a surrender of the fort and island to His Britannic Majesty's forces.[2] This, Sir,

1 The Post surgeon.

2 As to the difference in the hour which appears in these three official statements, it is probable each writer had in mind some different stage of the event. The question of the surrender of the island had its preliminary stage at an earlier hour in the morning at the old distillery at the western end of the village, between some of the British officers and certain of the citizens, while the formal demand on the post was not made until later in the day. And, again, Captain Roberts may have noted the time of writing his demand at his own headquarters and Lieut. Hanks the time it reached his hands.

was the first information I had of the declaration of war. I, however, had anticipated it, and was as well prepared to meet such an event as I possibly could have been with the force under my command, amounting to fifty-seven effective men, including officers. Three American gentlemen, who were prisoners, were permitted to accompany the flag. From them I ascertained the strength of the enemy to be from nine hundred to one thousand strong, consisting of regular troops, Canadians and savages; that they had two pieces of artillery, and were provided with ladders and ropes for the purpose of scaling the works, if necessary.[1] After I had obtained this information I consulted my officers, and also the American gentlemen present, who were very intelligent men; the result of which was, that it was impossible for the garrison to hold out against such a superior force. In this opinion I fully concurred, from the conviction that it was the only measure that could prevent a general massacre. The fort and garrison were accordingly surrendered.

. . . .

"In consequence of this unfortunate affair, I beg leave, Sir, to demand that a Court of Inquiry may be ordered to investigate all the facts connected with it; and I do further request, that the Court may be

1 A discrepancy in the estimate of troops as made by opposing sides, especially in reports from the battle field, is very common. A recent History of Canada, however (published in 1897), is inexcusably out of the way, when it makes Captain Roberts' attacking force "less than two hundred," as far as *voyageurs* and regulars were concerned, and makes no mention whatever of the large number of Indian allies.

specially directed to express their opinion on the merits of the case.

"PORTER HANKS,
"*Lieutenant of Artillery.*"

"His Excellency GEN. HULL,
"*Commanding the N. W. Army.*"

It is not necessary to discuss the question whether the surrender at Fort Mackinac, without a show of resistance, was justifiable. The garrison was but a handful of men. By no fault of his, the Lieutenant in command had been taken entirely unawares. The enemy were in overwhelming numbers and occupying a position with their cannon which commanded the fort. Their Indian allies were waiting in savage eagerness for the attack, and had the fighting once begun it would have been beyond the power of the officers to restrain them.[1]

The capture of Mackinac, the first stroke of the war, was of the highest importance to the British interests. Valuable stores of merchandise, as well as considerable shipping which stood in the harbor, were secured. It gave them the key to the fur trade of a vast region, and the entire command of the upper lakes. It exposed Detroit and all lower Michigan. It greatly terrified General Hull, who commanded the department of Michigan. It arrested his operations in Canada. He said: "The whole northern hordes of Indians will be let down upon

[1] John Askin, of the British storekeeping department, and present with the besieging force, said, that had the soldiers of the fort fired a gun, he firmly believed not a soul of them would have been saved.

us." His surrender, just one month later, was in part due to the panic it caused — one historian of that day, saying: "Hull was conquered at Mackinac."

On the island, the British proceeded at once to strengthen their position. In order to guard against any approach in the rear, like the successful one they themselves had made, they built a very strong earth-

THE PERRY CANNON.

work on the high hill, a half mile, or little more, back of the post, which they called Fort George, in honor of the King of England. This fortification still remains, now known to all visitors as Fort Holmes. In its construction the citizens of the village were impressed, every able bodied man being required to give three days in the pick and shovel work.

A common error prevails that this ancient earthwork was actually constructed the very night the British arrived, and that it made part of the formidable investment of Fort Mackinac which led to its speedy surrender. A moment's reflection will show this could not have been the case. The invading force only landed at three o'clock that morning and then, with all their trappings, had to march two miles to get into position, and yet were ready by ten o'clock to open fire. It is probable this hill was the "heights above the fort," to which, as Captain Roberts says in his report, "one of those unwieldy guns was brought up with much difficulty;" and that far the Fort Holmes' site figured in the demonstration against Lieut. Hanks' command. The fortification itself, however, being the scientific work of military engineers, and involving a protracted period of hard labor, was constructed afterwards at the British commandant's leisure. The other one of Captain Roberts' "two six-pounders," together with the great bulk of his men, including his Indians, we may suppose, occupied the ridge of ground, part open and part wooded, between the hill and the post, just beyond the old parade ground, which lies outside the present fort fence.

Captain Roberts was relieved, September, 1813, and Captain Bullock appointed in his place. Col. McDouall assumed charge in the spring of 1814. This officer's name often appears as McDonall.

CHAPTER VI

By Commodore Perry's victor on Lake Erie, and General Harrison's victorious battle of the Thames, the autumn of 1813 found the Americans in possession of Lake Huron, and nearly all of Michigan. The re-capture of Mackinac was determined on. In the early spring of 1814, an expedition for this purpose was planned, which, however, did not get under sail until July 3rd, embarking from Detroit that day. It was a joint naval and military force. There were seven war vessels under Commodore Sinclair, and a land force of 750 men, under command of Col. Croghan. The object, besides the retaking of Mackinac, was also to destroy the English post at St. Joseph, and to inflict whatever damage it could on the military stores and shipping of the enemy on the neighboring border of Canada. These war brigs and other vessels of the squadron were the largest ever seen, up to that time, on the waters of St. Clair and Huron. The commanders, instead of sailing at once to Mackinac, concluded to first dispatch their other errands. They found St. Joseph already abandoned by the British, but they captured some English schooners and other property, and continued their incursion as far as the Sault where they destroyed a large amount of supplies — Major Holmes being in charge of the expedition. They then turned back for Mackinac.

The English fully appreciated the great value, strategically and commercially, of Mackinac, and were determined to hold it. They took strong measures for its defense. Col. McDouall, who had been sent there in May of that year as the new commandant, was a very energetic and skillful soldier. He brought with him fresh troops from Canada, ammunition and provisions, and other things needful. Besides this fact, the garrison were by no means ignorant of the expedition in these northern waters, and of its object; and there was no possibility of a surprise attack. One of the officers belonging to the reinforcement which had been sent to the post thus wrote: "After our arrival at the island all hands were employed strengthening the defences of the fort. For upwards of two months half the garrison watched at night against attack." The Indians from the surrounding country, and Canadians here and there, were called in for aid. Besides the additional fort which they had built, Fort George (now Fort Holmes, and already referred to), batteries were placed at various points outside the walls which commanded the approaches to the beach. One was on the height overlooking the ground in front of the present Grand Hotel, another on the high knoll just west of the fort, while others lined the east bluff between the present fort grounds and Robinson's Folly.

Our American officers at first thought of erecting a battery on Round Island and shelling the fort from there. A yawl was sent with a squad of men to reconnoitre, and a spot fixed upon. This was seen by the English commander and he immediately sent over a large detachment of Indians, who forced the little party to flee. One of the men, however, waited too long, tempted by the berries which grew at his feet, and missed the boat and was captured. The Indians rowed in with their prisoner, chanting the death dirge and expecting to dispose of him on the shore in their usual barbaric manner; and in their wild frenzy of delight, some of the squaws, before the canoe had touched the beach, rushed into the water, waist deep, with whetted knives raised aloft, to begin at once the work of savage torturing. But the officer of the fort, divining their object, had sent a squad of soldiers to protect the hapless prisoner.

The extended level ground just west of the village streets was also considered as a point where a landing could be made, and the taking of the fort be attempted, under cover of the guns of the vessels. But Captain Sinclair, who described the fort hill as a "perfect Gibraltar," found that his vessels would only be exposed to a raking fire from the heights above without his being able to elevate his guns sufficiently for return shots.

After hovering about the island for a week it was concluded there was no other way than to imitate the plan of the successful enemy, two years before. So they sailed around to "British Landing" and disembarked, August 4th, and marched as far as the Dousman farm (now Early's farm). But the conditions were entirely different from those of two years ago, and the movement was ill-starred, and a melancholy failure. According, however, to the reports made by the joint commanders of the expedition, it was not so much their plan to attempt the storming of the works, as to feel the enemy's strength and to establish a lodgment from which by slow and gradual approaches, and by siege, they might hope for success. All such expectations were soon dissipated. Facing the open field on the Dousman farm were the thick woods. This was a perfect cover to the Indian skirmishers, who, concealed in their vantage points, hotly attacked our soldiers; to say nothing of an English battery of four pieces, firing shot and shells. There could be neither advance nor encamping. The only wise thing was to retreat to the vessels. This was done and the expedition left the island, having lost fifteen killed and about fifty wounded. Major Andrew Hunter Holmes, next in command to Colonel Croghan, was one of the slain in this most unfortunate and fruitless action. He fell while leading his battalion in a flank movement on the right. One story is that the gun which pierced his breast with two balls was fired by a little Indian boy. Another tradition is that the Major had been warned that morning, by a civilian aboard the vessel, not to wear his uniform, which would make him a target, but that he declined the friendly advice saying, that if it was his day to fall he was ready.[1]

Major Holmes was a Virginian, an intelligent and promising young officer who enjoyed the friendship of Thomas Jefferson. He had already distinguished himself in a battle near Detroit, and had performed well a special service assigned him in this same expedition, when at the Sault St. Marie. In the official reports of the Mackinac battle he was referred to as that " gallant officer, Major Holmes, whose character is so well known to the war department; " and again

1 Charles J. Ingersoll in "*Sketch of the Second War*," vol. 2.

as "the valuable and ever-to-be lamented officer." His body had been carried off the field and secreted by a faithful negro servant, and the next day was respectfully delivered to the Americans by Colonel McDouall and taken to Detroit for burial. A very fitting tribute to his memory was it, that when in the following year the island again came under our flag, the name of the new fort on the summit heights, which had been built by the English, was changed from Fort George to Fort Holmes.

The fort being found impregnable by assault, no further attempts at capture were made, and the expedition returned down the lake to Detroit, the most of the soldiers being sent to join General Brown's forces on the Niagara.

But the ambition to regain the island was not yet abandoned. It was thought to starve out the garrison and thus force a surrender. English supplies could now come only from Canada through the Georgian Bay. Near the mouth of the Nottawasaga river at the southeast corner of that bay, under a protecting block house, was the schooner "Nancy" loaded with six months' supplies of provisions intended for the Mackinac fort. A detachment of the American troops landing there blew up the block house and destroyed the schooner and her supplies. There remained now nothing more to do than to so guard the waters that the destitution of the island could not be repaired. Two of the vessels, the "Tigress" and the "Scorpion," were left to maintain a strict blockade. This was proving very effective, and provisions ran so low in Mackinac, that a loaf of bread would sell for a dollar on the streets, and the men of the garrison were killing horses for meat.

The following extract from a letter written by one of the English officers depicts the situation within the fort at this time: "After the failure of the attack, the Americans established a blockade by which they intercepted our supplies. We had but a small store of provisions. The commander grew very anxious. The garrison was put on short allowances. Some horses that happened to be on the island were killed and salted down, and we occasionally were successful in procuring fish from the lake. To economize our means the greater part of the Indians were induced to depart to their homes. At length we saw ourselves on the verge of starvation with no hope of relief from any quarter."

During all the summer we find Colonel McDouall in his letters to the department begging and entreating for supplies.

There were yet other embarrassments. Although throughout the whole period the Indians of the Mackinac region were allies of the British, the alliance was not without its difficulties. Many of them showed an indecision when success was doubtful, as one of the English agents wrote, and "a predilection in favor of the Americans seemed to influence them." About the island "they became very clamorous," another officer said. And Col. McDouall spoke of them as "an uncertain quantity"— that they "were fickle as the wind and it was a difficult task to keep them with us." He was embarrassed, too, by their flocking to the island and requiring to be fed.

But relief, and that by their own sagacity and daring, was at hand for the beleaguered garrison. When the " Nancy " and the block house on the Nottawasaga were destroyed, the officer in charge of that supply of stores, Lieut. Worsley, with seventeen sailors of the Royal Navy, had managed to escape and effect a passage in an open boat to the fort at Mackinac and had reported the loss of the stores. Forced by the necessity of the situation, a bold and desperate project was undertaken — that was, the capture of the two blockading vessels. Batteaux were fitted out and equipped at Mackinac, manned under Lieut. Worsley with his seamen and by volunteers from the garrison and Indians, making in all about seventy men. These set forth on the bold errand. The Scorpion and Tigress were then cruising in the neighborhood of Detour. On a dark night, rowing rapidly and in silence, they approached first the Tigress, which lay at anchor off St. Joseph, and taking it entirely by surprise, leaped aboard and after a hand to hand struggle soon had possession. Its crew were sent next day, as prisoners to Mackinac. The Tigress's signals were in the hands of the captors, and the American pennant was kept flying at the mast-head. On the second day after, the Scorpion was seen beating up towards her companion ship unaware of its change of fortune. Night coming on she anchored some two miles off. About daylight the Tigress set all sail, swept down on her, opened fire and boarded and captured her. Sad fate, indeed, for these two war vessels, which only a year before had honorably figured in Commodore Perry's victory on Lake Erie. I prefer not to dwell on the mortifying bit of history, except to say that candor and justice compel our highest admiration for this English feat of daring and prowess.

This ended all attempts to dislodge the English from our island. It remained under their flag until terms of peace and settlement were secured by the treaty of Ghent, February, 1815. Mackinac was ever a favorite point in the eyes of the British, and all along an object of their strong desire; and they were loath to give it up. Col. McDouall, the able and successful commandant, spoke with strong feeling of the "unfortunate cession of the fort and the island of Michilimackinac to the United States." It had been a matter of official complaint and criticism in the province of Upper Canada, that after the first war it had been "injudiciously ceded" by the English government. John Jay, our American representative in the conference of the treaty and the boundary lines, found that the commissioners of the Crown were more interested in an "extended commerce than in the possession of a vast tract of wilderness." The fur trade of that time was the main thing and Mackinac was the gateway to all the fur traffic of the west and southwest fields. And again, it appears in negotiating the treaty of 1815 that the commissioners of the crown, even when feeling obliged to forego a large part of their demands, still held out for the island of Mackinac (and Fort Niagara) as long as possible.[1] Thirty-two years had now passed since the American right to the island had been acknowledged by the treaty of 1783. Of these years only three had been years of war. But

[1] Henry Adams' "*History of the United States*," vol. 9, p. 34.

for one-half of that whole period the British flag had been flying over Fort Mackinac. In the complete sense, therefore, the destiny of the northwest was not assured until the treaty of Ghent.[1] With that treaty the question was finally and conclusively settled.

The posts of the English which had been captured

AMERICAN FUR CO. OLD SCALES.

by us, and ours here and there, which they had taken, were to be restored by each government to the other. In connection with this mutual delivery is an interesting fact mentioned in a private letter which Colonel McDouall wrote to his friend and fellow officer of the English army, Captain Bulger. He says that in the equipment of Fort Mackinac, at the time he

[1] Hinsdale's "*Old Northwest,*" p. 185.

was making the transfer, were cannon bearing the inscriptions: "Taken at Saratoga;" "Taken from Lord Cornwallis," and other such, and he speaks of his chagrin in being obliged to include, in his restoration of the fort, guns which told of English defeat and humiliation in the Revolutionary war; and that as an Englishman he felt "a strong temptation to a breach of that good faith which in all public treaties it is infamy to violate."

Surely it adds to our antiquarian and patriotic interest in the old fort to know that guns, captured from Burgoyne and from Cornwallis in the battles of the Revolution, once held position on these ramparts.

We do not know how these honorable trophies of the Revolution ever found their way to our remote pioneer out-post. We do know, however, that our loss of the fort, three years before, explains how they got back, temporarily, to their former English ownership. And now in their alternations of estate, after taking part in keeping off American troops from the island, and thus, as it were, redeeming themselves in English eyes from the bad fortune incurred in our war for independence, they again fell into our hands. And we can appreciate Col. McDouall's sense of regret at having to give them up. It was the same sentiment which Capt. McAfee, in his narrative of that war in which he himself had a part, tells us was exhibited by some of the British officers when by Hull's surrender several brass cannon fell to their hands which our forces had captured in the war of the Revolution — they "saluted them with tears."[1]

1 "*History of the Late War in the Western Country.*"

It is vain to surmise the history of those interesting guns subsequent to 1815. How long they remained at the island post, and whether in time they were sent to the smelter's furnace, or are still in honorable preservation somewhere with other war relics, we cannot say. In this connection it may be well to remark concerning that old fashioned cannon which has been lying in position on the village beach in front of the "fort garden," a familiar object for generations past. The story is that the gun figured in Com. Perry's battle on Lake Erie, though whether one of his own guns in the action or a British gun which he captured is uncertain; that it was left here long ago by one of the government revenue vessels. That it was put in charge of the Mackinac Custom House, and that it used to serve on 4th of July and other national occasions which called for celebration "at the cannon's mouth."

Although the treaty of Ghent had been made in December, 1814, by which the island reverted to the United States, yet so long were the dispatches in reaching the post, that hostilities were continuing in its vicinity for three or four months after peace had been declared.[1]

The instructions to McDouall were that he withdraw as soon as possible after July 1st, as occupation by the American troops was authorized by the 15th of that month. The withdrawal was delayed by the difficulty of deciding where to go. The British officers desired a locality near the boundary line, which would be suitable for a military post and by

[1] Likewise the battle of New Orleans was fought nearly a month after the treaty of peace had been made.

which, at the same time, they could favorably compete for control of the route between the upper and lower lakes. Added to this was the desire to maintain their hold on the Indians, and to secure all possible advantage in the fur commerce.

While the general boundary line of division, as respects the northern end of Lake Huron, had been agreed on by the American and British authorities, yet in respect to every individual island which bordered on that line of water, it had not then been definitely determined. But time pressed and the British authorities were compelled to decide on a spot; and an island, answering well in point of locality and very suitable in all physical features as a place of fortification, and presumably within the British line, was chosen. It lies about two miles off from Detour of the northern peninsula of Michigan at the entrance of the St. Mary's river connecting with Lake Superior. The Indian name it then bore was *Pontaganipy*. Afterward it became known as Drummond island, so called, it is presumed, in honor of Sir Gordon Drummond, at that time commander of the British forces in Canada.

Although the place was now determined on, further delay was occasioned by the scarcity of boats to effect the removal. And in the meantime a detachment of American troops under Col. Anthony Butler had arrived from Detroit to receive the fort. They came with a margin of time in advance of the stipulated 15th, and went into camp on the level field below the fort. The British commandant was obliged to request a short extension of time as the transportation facilities were not yet complete. This was courteously accorded, but there is a story to the effect that the American officers insisted on unfurling the stars and stripes over their camp on the ground below, when the 15th arrived — the British still occupying the fort.

On the British leaving, Col. Butler took command, but soon resigned it to Major Willoughby Morgan, who, within a few months, was succeeded by Col. Chambers.

CHAPTER VII

The relinquishment of the straits by the British troops, and their retirement to Drummond Island, and establishing a post there, and the strained relations between them and their American neighbors at Mackinac — all this forms a passage of some historical interest not unmixed with a comic element.

At Drummond Island Col. McDouall began military fortifications on an extensive plan with the fond dream of establishing a commanding military and commercial center. The new post was only some forty miles from Mackinac. The garrisons were men of the same blood and language. They were neighbors and each the only near neighbor the other had. Peace prevailed between the two flags, and we might have thought of amity and fellowship in that remote wilderness of water and forest. But it was not long before relations became strained and letters of crimination and recrimination went back and forth. One question pertained to the ownership of Round Island, lying just in front of Mackinac — the American authorities at the post choosing to ignore a deed of cession thereof made by the Indians to a certain individual of Mackinac village during the recent British control. But for the most part the grounds of dispute were so trifling and imaginary that the ebullitions of excited feeling seem now almost amusing. The Indians going back and forth, and seeking favors on each island, made mischief with their tongues. The white traders, too, in both places may have fomented the strife. A few of the villagers, sympathizing more or less with the English cause, or having kindred among the Drummond people, had remained at Mackinac, where their homes and property were. Tales were reported of their being wronged, and subjected to indignities, and their business interfered with, and of one person in particular, the wife of a man who had gone to Drummond, being threatened as a "British spy;" and it was excitedly declared that there was "more liberty in Algeria than at present in Michilimackinac." Col. McDouall, influenced by the exaggerated reports, wrote to the island authorities in a protesting and rather offensive tone. Putoff, the Mackinac agent of Indian affairs, sent back a hot reply. In language emphatic, but not always elegant, he denied the allegations made of any injustice or indignity having been shown; and in reference to the "spy" charge that the party declared she had never heard she was thus accused, that she stands ready "to confront your informant and," to use her own phraseology, 'Give him the *Lye!*'"

The writer then makes counter-charges and claims that according to reports brought by the Indians from Fort Drummond, Col. McDouall was endeavoring to interfere with Mackinac trade; that he had held a council with the Indians, and warned them against the Americans who proposed inviting them to Mackinaw for the purpose of secretly massacring them; that "red wampum and tobacco mixed with vermillion" (the symbol of war) had been distributed; that barrels of rum were opened to inflame

LESLIE AVENUE.

their animosity; and they were again urged to grasp the tomahawk, and that he himself was purposing soon to return with his big guns and recapture Mackinac.

To this Col. McDouall replies; in his dignity, however, refusing to again communicate with the Indian Agent, but addressing his letter to Col. Chambers, the commandant at the fort. He laughs at what he calls "the absurd stories" of the Indians, and the "precious tissue of abominable lies." He denies advising them against American trade. The charges that he had warned them against going to Mackinac lest they should be entrapped and destroyed, and had advised them to take up the tomahawk against the Americans and that he himself was planning an attack on their island, were idle tales. As to the barrels of rum, not even a glassful had been given, "so economically was the council conducted," he says. No wampum of a red kind or any other color had been distributed, nor had there been "the most distant allusion which malice could torture into the indication of approaching war." And the "minute guns" which had figured as a warlike tocsin in the story carried to Mackinac he explained, with a glowing British pride, was a royal salute fired in honor of the victory of Wellington at Waterloo over Napoleon, "the greatest despot that ever waded through slaughter to a throne." This was in 1815, it will be remembered, two or three months after Waterloo; and it is interesting to find that away out in the northernmost waters of Lake Huron, remote from all other seats of habitation, this event in European history was duly celebrated by the resounding guns.

And so the poor Indians appear for the once as practical jokers at the expense of the superior race; telling "cock and bull" stories, now to one island and then to the other. There is a blending of the comical and pathetic in the thought of these poor children of the forest, so often the football of the whites, proving such serious mischief-mongers and stirring up so much bad blood between the two bands of their conquerors — as it were "playing off one against the other."

We continue this story only to say that the high expectations in regard to Drummond Island as a British post, influential in Indian affairs and in the commerce along the American border, were doomed to disappointment. McDouall was not allowed to develop, except to a very limited extent, his plans of military fortifications, nor to realize his fond dream of making it a great commercial seat. He remained in command only for one year after leaving Mackinac, and returned to England, it is said, a disappointed man.[1] This disappointment marked the subsequent history of Drummond Island as a British seat. For, some years after settling there the joint commissioners conferring concerning a few questions which still lingered between Canada and

[1] This British officer commands our respect for his high abilities. From his published letters he seems to have been a man of literary culture, and capacity for state craft as well as military training. He attained the rank of Major-General, and lived until 1848, having entered the army in 1796. Kingsford in his "*History of Canada*," vol. 8, speaks of him as a "zealous and active officer, whose performance of the duties entrusted to him has entitled him to the most honorable mention."

the United States respecting the division line in the island-studded part of upper Lake Huron and the river St. Mary, decided that that part of the lake in which Drummond Island lay belonged to the United States side of the line. Accordingly in 1828 the British garrison removed and the island was turned over to our government.[1]

To return now to our Island post in the straits. The American spirit and regime were soon fully restored after its re-possession by our troops in 1815. From that time on there was a long succession of regular army soldiers and officers inhabiting the old quarters and barracks. Many of the officers who afterwards acquired high rank and distinction during our civil war, 1861–1865, either in the Union Army or Southern, had been in service here as young Captains or Lieutenants. Among them were Gen. Sumner, Gen. Heintzelman, Gen. Kirby Smith, Gen. Silas Casey, and Gen. Fred Steele, for whom a fort in the west has been named. General Pemberton was once a member of the garrison, and in a private letter written by one of the citizens in 1840, when the little island was ice-bound and there was a dearth of news, it is incidentally mentioned that "Lieut. Pemberton in the fort is engaged in getting up a private theatre, in an endeavor to ward off winter and solitude,"—the young officer little dreaming of that more serious drama in which he was to act, twenty-three years

[1] Samuel F. Cook, of Lansing, Mich., has written a most interesting sketch of Drummond Island — giving the story of its occupation and final abandonment by the British; giving also some of the fascinating legendary lore which has gathered about the spot. The sketch is embellished with numerous photographic views.

later, as commander of Vicksburg, with Grant's besieging army around him.

During the civil war, all troops being needed at the front, the soldiers were withdrawn from our fort. This was but temporary, however, and did not mean its abandonment.[1] Its flag and a solitary serjeant were left to show that it was still a military post of the United States. This faithful soldier remained at the fort for many years after the war, and was known to the visitors as the "Old Serjeant." For a period during the war it was made the place of confinement of some of the Confederate prisoners, principally notable officers who had been captured, at which time Michigan volunteer troops held it.

At the close of the war the fort resumed its old time service as a garrison post, generally about fifty or sixty men of the regular army, with their officers, composing the force. A detachment would serve a few years, then be transferred and another would take its place, to enjoy in its turn the recuperative climate of the summer, and to endure the rigors and the isolation of the winters. So the old fort continued in use, with its morning and evening gun, its stirring bugle notes, its daily "guard mount," its pacing sentry, its drill, its "inspection days," until 1895. Then the sharp and decisive voice of authority called "halt" to the long march of military history in the straits of Mackinaw. The United States government, by formal act of Congress, abandoned the fort, and gave it over, together with the National Park of

[1] Occasionally at other times, also, the garrison would be temporarily sent elsewhere, but this never meant the giving up of the post.

eleven hundred acres, to the State of Michigan. The fort was dismantled, the old cannon were removed from the walls, and every soldier withdrawn. We do not question the fact, that as a fort constructed in primitive times it was unsuited to the days of modern warfare; nor the fact that with the numerous other well equipped posts the department is maintaining for its troops, this old-fashioned one was not an absolute necessity. Nor do we question for a moment the propriety of making the State of Michigan the legatee and successor to this property, if the general government was determined to dispossess itself of it. It could not have been more suitably bestowed, if it had to pass into other hands. The commissioners, to whose charge it is now committed, appreciate and will cherish that historic and patriotic interest which attaches to the old fort, and will keep the grounds intact and carefully guard the buildings. They will aim likewise to preserve the trees and the drives of the park in that natural beauty which has so long given them such charm. But while thus assured, it is at the same time a matter of deep regret that the national government should have forsaken the island. For sentimental reasons alone, even had there been no other, the old fort should have been retained as a United States post. A military seat which has two hundred years or more of history behind it, is not often to be found in the western world. Indeed, with the possible exception of Fort Marion, the old Spanish fortification at St. Augustine, Fla., it is doubtful if there be another on this whole continent, which could boast of so long a period of continuous occupation as old Fort Michilimackinac, which was established first at St. Ignace in the 17th century, then removed to old Mackinaw, and since 1780 has been located on our island.

The Legislature of Michigan in the Spring of 1897, by formal act made the offer of recession to the United States of the old military post with all the garrison buildings and all the ground known as the Fort and Military reservation; such transfer to be made whenever the War Department should notify the commissioners of its readiness to accept the tender. This would still leave what is known as the Park in the hands of the State of Michigan. By reason of the enlargement of the army, and the need there will be for additional barracks and quarters for our soldiers, and because of the eminent fitness and suitability of the Island for an army post it is thought the U. S. Government may incline to this offer, and that the old historic fort may again be occupied.

CHAPTER VIII

It is interesting to think of the progressive series of industries, as pertaining to the welfare of man, in connection with the vast stretches of land in our New America. First of all was the hunting and trapping of the wild animals of the wilderness. Their flesh served the early aborigines of the forest for food, and their skins for clothing. But the Indians' operations of this kind were but a slight and insignificant prelude to what developed with the coming of the whites, particularly in our northern and western wilds. With their advent the great fur trade began. The forests and the soil of these millions of acres were of importance only as being the lairs and roaming grounds of those fur-bearing creatures, large and small, which for

THE SHORE DRIVE.

nearly two centuries made a great element in the world's commerce. Only the slightest part of the immense captures was availed of for food. The skins of the animals were the sole object sought. For these, great companies organized and wrought and developed into well nigh imperial power in the wilderness tracts.

Following this era the forests themselves, so long the homes of the animals and the scene of their slaughter, became a most valuable element in our western settlements by the development of the lumber trade, connecting with human habitations and a higher form of social life. Then the soil itself, which for centuries had been covered by these dense forests, served another end in the interest of man by its trees giving way to the plow. The last form of industrial development in connection with the land has to do with "the earth beneath." The fur-bearing animals to a great extent gone, the forests largely a thing of the past, the surface of the earth occupied and tilled, the enterprise of man delves below and brings up the long hidden treasures of ore and coal and oil which prove such mighty factors in modern civilization.

The fur trade was a pioneer industry in North America. Its agents were the first to penetrate the primeval wilderness in the name of commerce, and in this sense were the precursors of civilization. They made distant and perilous journeys, and were often the first to reveal some solitary river or lake or new stretch of land. Their camps and petty forts became the outposts of colonizers, and to them is largely due the earlier opening to the civilized world of the unknown and inhospitable "regions beyond." The history of the fur trade is thus the history of exploration and occupation, with its own heroes and adventures and annals. By stimulating hunting and turning it into a sort of forest labor it served to create an industry among the Indians, though at the same time it diminished the animals upon which the tribes depended for subsistence and, most unfortunately, introduced among them the evil of ardent spirits.

The countries of Europe, together with our seaboard states, were the market fields, and from the whole vast regions of our Northwest, whence now go the cargoes of grain, there then "went east," in the line of commerce, only the packs of peltry. The animals that were hunted for their fur were principally the following (as far at least as the more northern fields were concerned), the order in which they are named indicating the relative amount of supply by the various species: beaver, marten (sable), muskrat, lynx, fox, otter, wolf, bear, mink, deer, buffalo and racoon. Sir Alexander Mackenzie, writing concerning the fur trade in the British possessions of the Northwest, and probably speaking only for the one company which he represented (the Northwestern) reported for one year the number of furred animals taken as 182,000, of which 106,000 were beavers.

While fur-trading in America was practiced to some extent in the early days of the Dutch on the Hudson, its magnitude of operations, its longer continuance, its influence on governments and on civilization, and its romance withal, belong rather to the business as conducted in the western half of North

America — more particularly in the Northern and Northwestern parts. From the earliest settlements of the French in Canada the fur trade ranked as of first importance. "Beaver skins were the life of New France," it was said. But the greatest development of the business was at the hands of the Hudson's Bay Company; a company chartered by King Charles II. in 1670, and which in process of time acquired a fur trade territory more than half as large as all Europe, extending from the Arctic Circle to the Red River on the South, and west to the Pacific Coast. While their territory was afterwards sold and transferred to the Dominion of Canada,[1] yet the Company as a business corporation has existed for fully two centuries and still continues its operations, and is perhaps the earliest link now left connecting business interests of to-day with the remote past. For more than a century the great Company had flourished without much competition. Then a formidable rivalry developed. About 1787, the Northwest Fur Company took shape, and became a very powerful organization, "the mighty Northwesters" its people were called. Washington Irving wrote of it: "It held a lordly sway over the wintry lakes and boundless forests of the Canadas, almost equal to that of the East India Company over the realms of the Orient."[2]

The principal partners resided in Montreal and Quebec, and constituted a commercial aristocracy, and in their relation to the various grades of the

[1] This was in 1869, when their territory of 2,300,000 square miles was transferred to the Canadian Government.

[2] Astoria, Chapter 1.

hundreds in their employ, the old feudal and fief idea seemed restored. Every year a delegation of these magnates would journey to their wilderness headquarters at Fort William, on the north shore of Lake Superior, where a conference was held with the inferior partners and agents from the various outlying trading posts. They travelled in large palatial canoes equipped with every convenience and luxury possible, taking with them their own cooks and bakers, and delicacies of every kind. With business they combined pleasure in their sojourn at Fort William, and in the halls of the Council house regaled themselves with banquets and revels.[1]

Besides having the territory of the Canadas for its operations, the new company stretched its lines indefinitely to regions beyond and, as was inevitable, when reaching the border lands they clashed in trade jealousy with the Hudson's Bay Co. The mutual strife and animosity were very bitter and long continued. Removed far beyond the reach of civilization they were a law unto themselves, and deeds of violence and slaughter were common. The Northwest Company in time extended its operations into United States territory. Indeed, up to the beginning of the 19th century the whole of the fur trade in America, with the exception of that of the Russians in Alaska, was a British monopoly. We have already seen how slowly and reluctantly the treaty of 1783, as respects these northern latitudes, was recognized by the British Government. British traders pre-

[1] "The opulence of the Lake Superior fur trade in the closing days of the 18th Century can be compared with the opulence of the Lake Superior copper trade in the closing days of the 19th Century." Moore's "*The Northwest Under Three Flags.*"

tended to regard all this country as still in some sense belonging to the throne, or at least that the boundary question was an open one; and as the conflict of 1812 was approaching they used to tell the Indians that that war would settle it. The war did settle it, but not as they had imagined. The new adjudication of the boundary question left it just as it had been determined by the treaty following the war of the revolution.[1]

Michilimackinac, when a fort on the mainland, had from an early day been a depot for furs. The French military governor, or commandant, held a supervisory and fostering relation to the business. This was continued by the English when by their conquest of Canada their flag waved over the Straits. Traders established themselves within the palisades of the fort enclosure to barter with the Indians — cloth, beads, knives, powder and rum passing in exchange for the peltries brought in from the woods. With the removal of the fort from the mainland to our island of Mackinac the fur trade continued, though with the change from the custom which had prevailed before that no longer were the traders allowed to have their business, their homes, their church and their whole community life within the fort enclosure. They thus formed a settlement at the foot of the fort hill which developed into the village of

[1] Mrs. Jameson, of England, in recounting her travels in Canada (1837) relates: "Colonel Talbot (of Canada), told me that when he took a map, and pointed out to one of the English Commissioners the foolish bargain they had made, the real extent, value and resources of the countries ceded to the United States, the man covered his eyes with his clenched hands, and burst into tears."

Mackinac. The Mackinaw Fur Company was formed, and later the Southwestern Company took shape, both under British control.

The spirit of American enterprise began to assert itself. John Jacob Astor of New York, on a suggestion dropped by a chance fellow traveller on shipboard, had made a venture in Canadian peltries which proved very remunerative. This led to his embarking further into the business. It was not long before he secured a controlling interest in both of these companies. Besides conducting operations in the regions already familiar, Astor sought to establish an agency on the Pacific coast, a venturesome and unsuccessful enterprise minutely described by Washington Irving in his "Astoria." The competition of the British traders, particularly of the powerful Northwest Company, was found wherever Astor turned. And the war of 1812 naturally proved unfortunate for his business schemes. But his prospects were vastly improved at the close of the war by an act of Congress which prohibited all British traders or companies operating in the United States. The Northwest Company, which had been freely so doing, now found its establishment in those parts of little worth to its business. Astor went to Montreal and at almost his own price bought all their trading posts within the limits of the United States. Together with its posts, the Northwest Company transferred many of its experienced agents, clerks, interpreters, and boatmen. The rivalry between the two British Companies having now ceased, their old strife did not long continue. The Hudson's Bay Company and the Northwest settled their long-time feud by joining together, the latter giving up its name in that of the older association — the Hudson's Bay Company of two centuries ago.

Astor now had a free course. The two companies, the Mackinaw and the Southwest, which he already controlled, were merged under the popular name of the American Fur Company. The business of the company grew and assumed great proportions. It had its connections and dependencies throughout the regions of the Mississippi, the Missouri and the Yellowstone rivers as well as those nearer by.

Mackinac Island was the company's headquarters of operation, and the little village took on an almost metropolitan character. It was a great mart of trade long before Chicago, Milwaukee or St. Paul had entered on their first beginnings, and vied with its cotemporaries, Detroit and St. Louis. The capital and enterprise on the island pertained principally to the business of the Company. They furnished employment to a great number of men, who with their families largely contributed to the life of the village. In the summer, when for several weeks the agents and *voyageurs* (or canoe men) and the *engages* of different kinds gathered in from the widely scattered hunting and trading grounds of the wilderness, they made, together with the local contingent employed the year through, a force of some twenty-five hundred men, all representing the work of the great organization. The Company's warehouses, stores, offices and boat yards occupied much of the town plat. The present summer hotel, The John Jacob Astor, was originally built for their business, furnishing quarters for the housing of their men, particularly at the great summer gatherings, and also ware-rooms where the peltries were weighed and packed and kept in storage.

The American Fur Company continued to flourish at Mackinac for a period of some twenty years. In 1834 Mr. Astor sold his interest, and the business declined. At length the Company withdrew entirely from the island, and for the remainder of its career was simply an agency for handling furs in New York. Our island, in a commercial and social point of view, suffered greatly by this change. A considerable element of the population removed. Business fell off, though to an extent revived by the development of the fishery interests. The old warehouses and other quarters of the Company, once the scene of activity and bustle, stood only as mute witnesses to a former life until removed or reconstructed and put to other uses. Some of these buildings were depositories of old papers, account books, letters, memoranda, etc., of the defunct Company which, of no business value, had been left in closets and attic chests. The new owners of the buildings at length felt indisposed to longer give them "house room," and after more than a generation had passed, several large packing boxes, filled with these old documents, were opened and freely disposed of to any of the village people who cared to take them away. The historic or memorial interest not then being very strong, the papers were used in various ways, such as lighting fires or putting them around the garden cabbage plants as protection against the cut-worm or a summer frost, and in the kitchens of the good housewives they were serving to line cake-tins with.

In 1863, and again in 1870, portions of these old papers and record books, which by that time had become interesting relics, were rescued by an enthusiastic lady visitor on the island, and presented to the Chicago Historical Society. In the great fire which swept over that city in 1871, these collections were destroyed. In the Astor House on the island there

OLD FUR COMPANY'S DESK.

are two large copy-volumes of letters written from the Company's office at Mackinac, and dating from a period the most flourishing in its history. These old books interest many of the summer guests to-day. Also belonging to the same Hotel, and preserved as relics, are an old fashioned high-legged desk at which one of the clerks used to work in the Company's palmy days, and an old-style scales or "balances," which was used in weighing the peltries as they were packed and bound for storage or for shipment.

CHAPTER IX

In the early days, even as in the present, the time of greatest stir and animation on the island was the summer season. Large companies of Indians from all quarters about the upper lakes would gather here. They came for the annuities from the government agent, and for trade and excitement — their wigwams lining up on the beach, two and three rows deep, their light canoes skimming the water or, with bottom turned up, resting on the pebbly shore. In some seasons as many as three thousand were present. Their unrestrained indulgence in liquor and their war dances and rude sport, added to all the so-called pleasurings of the Fur Company's *voyageurs* and trappers from the distant woods, made the island for a few weeks a constant scene of wildness. The hill-side fort, however, with its soldiers and frowning cannon had a salutary influence, while the business which the season brought to the merchants and the Indian traders probably served to relieve the situation.

The Indians were often but as babes in commercial transactions; and it is told of a certain settlement of them in the Grand Traverse Region, that coming to the island at such times they were often accompanied by their missionary, the Rev. Mr. Dougherty, a Presbyterian minister, who would pitch his tent among them during their stay, not only to guard their morals but to protect and assist them, as best he might, in their dealings with the traders.[1]

Another class of summer "tourists" and visitors on the island were the Fur Company's men, who would come in brigades of canoes with their collections of furs from the different trading posts in the wilderness, extending from the line of the British dominion in the north to the Missouri in the west, and to the south unto the confines of the white settlements. When all were thus assembled they added largely, for several weeks, to the white population of the village. About five hundred of them would be quartered in the Company's barracks, and others camped in tents, or were accommodated in the houses of the islanders. Joviality and frollicking and carousals were the order of the day among these light-hearted and improvident men who in a few summer weeks, amid the scenes of unaccustomed social life, would throw away their hard-earned wages of ten months' toil in the desolate wilds. As the early autumn approached they would gather the materials of another outfit, load their canoes, wave their good-

[1] As illustrating the obscurity and confusion attending an Indian's reasoning powers in business matters, Schoolcraft relates the following "claim" submitted to himself when Indian agent at Mackinac by a certain old Ottawa chief: At one time a trader had taken from him forty beavers; at another time thirty beavers and bears; at another, ten beavers; and at another, thirty beavers and four carcasses of beavers, for all which he had received no pay although promised it. Also, he had once served as a clerk or sub-trader for a merchant, for which he was to receive $500, and never got a cent of it. All this itemized "bill" he requested the President of the United States to pay! On inquiry it was found that the skins were sold, and the service rendered, and the wrong received some thirty or forty years before at Athabasca Lake, in the Hudson's Bay Territory, and far beyond the President's jurisdiction.

byes, and dipping their paddles to the rhythm of their boat-songs, gaily move off for another campaign in the distant regions of the wilderness.

These men were a class of their own. They were principally French Canadians, often with a mixture of Indian blood, who loved the free life of the water and the wilderness, and chafed under the restraints of settled society. Some of them in an earlier period had been known as *Couriers des bois,*— rangers of the woods. Of the same light-hearted, reckless and daring spirit they had been men of a little more responsibility than the ordinary *engague*. They were a kind of pedlars or sub-merchants on a small scale. Three or four would join their stock, put all in a canoe which they worked themselves, and push out into the wilderness to hunt and trap, and to barter with the Indians for furs, and after twelve or fifteen months' absence in the woods would return with rich cargoes, squander all their gains and then go back penniless to their favorite mode of life. They have been described as "grown up babes of the woods," on whom the dense and quiet forest tracts exercised a subtle fascination; and who felt the enticements of fur hunting much the same as our pioneer roving miners would feel the passion of gold hunting.[1] Later, however, when the great fur companies controlled all this business, there was little scope for these petty dealers, and the men of that type of life merged into the class known as *voyageurs*. The *voyageurs* were canoe men who handled the boats and worked them up the rapids in rivers and over por-

[1] "The hardy, adventurous, lawless, fascinating fur trade."—Parkman's "*The Old Regime in Canada.*"

tages. They were rough and bold and often as intractable as the Indians themselves, but of a cheerful and merry disposition,[1] devoid of ambition and contented under the privations and hardship of their life. Their food on their journeys was "lyed" corn, a sort of hominy, and salt pork, or in the absence of pork an allowance of tallow. This was greatly relished and gave them strength for their toils, better, it is said, than a diet of bread and fresh meat.[2]

The canoes used on these expeditions were fashioned on the model of the Indian canoe. They were made of birch-bark strippings a quarter of an inch in thickness, sewed together with fibres of spruce and made water-tight by hot pitch poured over the seams. The bark thus seamed together was stretched over thin ribs and cross bars of cedar. It was claimed that the white man had never been able to improve upon the original Indian idea. As intended for trading purposes, the canoes were often of great size, thirty or forty feet long and four to five feet wide. The ends were of gondola shape and often decorated with rude and gaudy paintings. They could carry, besides the crew of eight or ten men, four tons of freight, and yet in their construc-

1 The fiddle was a part of their camp outfit. They carried with them into the wilderness and wherever they went their "melodies of the river, the chase, love and wassail."—"*Wisconsin Collections*," vol. 14.

2 As giving some idea of the extent of this kind of navigation, we are told that in the palmy days of the Northwest Fur Company not less than ten brigades, of twenty canoes each, used to pass and repass every summer, between Montreal and Fort William on Lake Superior, carrying supplies to the upper country and returning with furs.

tion were very light and easily handled. These boats penetrated the recesses of the wilderness, not only following the rivers and every inlet, but "making a

THE SHORE DRIVE.

portage," as it was called, passing across land from one water highway to another. The portages were made by unloading the boat, which then (so light was its structure) could easily be carried on the shoulders of two of the men, while the packs of freight were strapped on the backs of the others.[1] Thus loaded, the cavalcade would march through thickets and swamps and over hills to the next sheet of water.

In the water the canoes were propelled, generally, by paddles made of the light red cedar, though in favorable winds a square sail might be hoisted. Later the American Fur Co. introduced oars. The rate of travel would average forty miles a day. After the fur trade declined and there was less call for the old lines of work, but more canoe journeying of a general kind, many of the old *voyageur* class became "masters of transportation" as it were, and "public carriers," on the upper lakes, in the days before steam navigation had fully developed its lines. The men were experts with the paddle, and capable of prolonged steady work, and the records sometimes made were astonishing. They could easily maintain a speed of four miles per hour for the whole day. Col. McKenney tells of thus journeying on these lakes in 1826, when his men had been one day paddling constantly since three o'clock in the morning. At sunset he proposed they go ashore for the night. But they assured him they were still fresh, and they continued at work until half past nine o'clock, which made a journey for the day of seventy-nine miles. While forty strokes a minute was a common rate of speed, they were capable of sixty, he says, and they placed the paddles in the water and took them out as noiselessly as if it had been oil. No duck moved

1 Of the smaller sized bark canoes — they were so light that after being unburdened the person who was the last to step out could take it by one of the thin ribs that crossed it midway and walk out with it upon the shore as if it were a basket.

on the surface of the water "with greater buoyancy or stillness, than do these birchen canoes." The motion was often accompanied by the notes of the Canadian boat songs sung by the crew, the measure and cadence of which would tally with the propelling strokes —

"Their voices kept tune,
And their paddles kept time." [1]

So charmed was the Colonel by his experiences in the canoe that he adopted as his own the sentiments of another enthusiast who had "dropped into poetry" on the subject — a few stanzas of which we venture to quote, admirable as a tribute at least, if not of the highest poetic merit:

"In the region of lakes where the blue waters sleep
Our beautiful fabric was built;
Light cedar supported its weight in the deep,
And its sides with the sunbeams were gilt.

"Its rim was with tender young roots woven round,
Like a pattern of wicker-work rare;
And it press'd on the waves with as lightsome a bound
As a basket suspended in air.

"The heavens in their brightness and glory below
Were reflected quite plain to the view,

[1] Isaac Weld, an English traveler in Canada, 1795–1797, describing his canoe journey tells of one instance when the men were kept at the paddles all night; and notwithstanding they had labored hard during the day, "they plied as vigorously as if they had just set out, singing merrily the whole time. The French Canadians have a good ear for music, and sing with tolerable accuracy. They have one favorite song among them called 'the rowing duet,' which as they sing they mark time to with each stroke of the oar; indeed, when rowing in smooth water, they mark the time of most of the airs they sing in the same manner." The singing, it was said, enabled them to paddle more steadily and keep better time.

And it moved like a swan — with as graceful a show,
Our beautiful birchen canoe.

"Oh, long will we think of those silver bright lakes,
And the scene they exposed to our view;
Our friends — and the wishes we formed for their sakes,
And our bright yellow birchen canoe."

Mrs. Jameson, from whom I have already quoted, and must yet again before this book is finished, describes her canoe journey through the Georgian Bay, made about ten years subsequent to McKenney's. "The Roman Emperor," she says, "who proclaimed a reward for the discovery of a new pleasure ought to have made a voyage down Lake Huron in a birch bark canoe." In her party there were two canoes, each twenty-five feet long and four feet in width, "tapering to the two extremities, and light, elegant and buoyant as the sea-mew when it skims the summer waves." Her *voyageurs* were Canadian half-breeds, "young, well-looking, full of glee and good nature, with untiring arms and more untiring lungs and spirits," and showing toward herself a never failing *gallanterie*." Their singing of the Canadian boat songs was very animated on the water and in the open air. They all sang in unison, raising their voices and marking the time with their paddles. Their progress over the water "was measured by pipes." At the end of a certain time there is a pause, "and they light their pipes and smoke for about five minutes, then the paddles go off merrily again at the rate of about fifty strokes in a minute and we absolutely seem to fly over the water. 'Trois pipes' are about twelve miles."[1] She was often amused by a

[1] "A French Canadian is scarcely ever without a pipe in his

specimen of dexterity on the part of her good natured cavalier men of the paddle "like that of an accomplished whip in London. They would paddle up toward the shore with such velocity that I expected to be dashed on the rock, and then in a moment, by a simultaneous back-stroke of the paddle, stop with a jerk, which made me breathless."

Another graphic canoeing picture of those times is given by H. H. Bancroft in the "North West Coast" of his series, "History of the Pacific States." It was as the *voyageurs* approached the end of their journey, he says, that they merged into their gayest mood. An elaborate toilet was made; men and boats were decorated with ribbons, tassels and gaudy feathers; the *chanson a l'aviron* (song of the oar) was struck and the plaintive paddling melody, which the distant listener might almost fancy to be the very voice of mountain, wood, and stream united, swelled on nearer approach into a hymn of manly exultation, and with flourish of paddle keeping time to song and chorus they swept round bend or point, and landed with a whoop and wild halloo. He describes it as a brilliant and stirring scene to "stand upon the bank and witness the arrival of a brigade of light canoes, dashing up with arrow-swiftness to the very edge of the little wharf; then, like a Mexican with his mustang, coming to a sudden stop, accomplished as if by

mouth, whether working at the oar or plough, whether on foot, or on horseback; indeed, so much addicted are the people to smoking that by the burning of the tobacco in their pipes they commonly ascertain the distance from one place to another. "Such a place," they say, "is three pipes off"—it is that far that you can smoke three pipes of tobacco in walking to it."—Isaac Weld, in his "*Travels Through the States of North America and Provinces of Canada in* 1795, '96, *and* '97."

miracle by backing water simultaneously, each with his utmost strength then rolling their paddles all together on the gunwale, shake from their bright vermilion blades a shower of spray, from which the rowers lightly emerge as from a cloud."

Or let us take one more description of this "homing" scene from the same writer: "Forty or sixty of these fantastically painted boats rushing through the water at reindeer speed under a cloud of flying spray toward their last landing, while in the breast of every tugging oarsman there were twenty caged hozannas which, rising faintly at first, were poured in song upon the breeze from five hundred tremulous tongues until finally, breaking all control, they would burst forth in one loud, long peal of triumphant joy."

CHAPTER X

In the year 1822 there occurred on the island an event which became famous in the annals of physiology and of medical experiment, both in this country and throughout Europe. This was the incident of Alexis St. Martin, who was accidentally wounded while handling a shot gun, and his treatment by Dr. Wm. Beaumont, the Post Surgeon. The accident happened in the retail store room of the American Fur Company. The room still stands; a basement or ground floor, a strong stone structure, over which was a second story built of logs. This upper story was afterwards removed, and an attractive white frame cottage with dormer windows is now to be seen built on the same high foundation walls which then made the store room. The building is situated near the foot of the Fort hill, on the corner of the street.

St. Martin was a young French Canadian in the employ of the American Fur Co. Mr. Gurdon S. Hubbard, a pioneer citizen of Chicago, at that time a young man living on the island, and present in the room when the accident occurred, thus wrote of it in his autobiography, published in 1888: "One of the party was holding a shot gun which was accidentally discharged, the whole charge entering St. Martin's body. The muzzle was not over three feet from him; I think not over two. The wadding entered, as well as pieces of his clothing; his shirt took fire; he fell, as we supposed, dead."

The shot had entered his side and perforated his stomach. Dr. Beaumont was immediately called and undertook the treatment of the wound. In his

DR. WILLIAM BEAUMONT.

report of the case, he says he found " a portion of the lung as large as a turkey's egg protruding from the external wound, lacerated and burnt, and immediately below this another protrusion, which proved to be a portion of the stomach, lacerated through all its coats and pouring out the food he had taken for his breakfast."

The man was healed and rounded out a good period of life. He became the father of a family and was able to serve in different forms of manual labor. Dr. Beaumont kept him in his employ long after he was healed for the purpose of conducting his valuable experiments, and at different intervals during a period of eleven years, at Fort Mackinac and at other army posts where he was stationed as surgeon, he made him the subject of painstaking study in the interest of medical science. He afterwards published a book detailing the whole case. The orifice into the stomach, about two and a half inches long, was purposely kept open, and through it as through a window (the man lying on his back as he took his food) Beaumont studied the processes of digestion, and the nature of the gastric juice — which he would extract through the aperture and then analyze and make experiments with. His range of experiments, covering nearly every article of food, afforded opportunity of determining the variations in their digestibility. And in his observations on St. Martin, who was not always in an amiable mood when thus being diagnosed (having to lie on his back while eating and sometimes required, "in the interest of science," to fast from twelve to eighteen hours) the Doctor noted the fact that anger and impatience retarded, or checked entirely, the digestive process!

The poor fellow was often irritable, not only as being the subject of these scientific experiments in which it is likely he had not himself the slightest interest (albeit it heralded his name throughout the medical world) but because also he was subject to the jibes of the populace. They called him "the man with the lid on his stomach," and made sport of him, and he was often provoked to resent their jeers in hot blood, with warnings to the Doctor about "giving up his job," and on one or two occasions peremptorily doing so. The surgeon had need of all his patience and tact in dealing with his interesting "study."

It was the first opportunity ever offered of an ocular examination of the interior of the human stomach in the moments of its functional work. During an examination, Dr. Beaumont says: "St. Martin swallowed part of a glass of water, and, being in a strong light, favorable to an internal view through the aperture, I distinctly saw the water pass into the cavity of the stomach through the cardiac orifice, a circumstance, perhaps, never before witnessed in a living subject. On taking repeated draughts of water, while in this position, it would gush out at the aperture the instant it passed through the cardia. Food swallowed in this position could be distinctly seen to enter the stomach."

Thus, he tells us in the preface of the book, "the secretions and operations of the stomach have been submitted to my observation in a very extraordinary manner, in a state of perfect health and for years in succession;" that the case presented "a concurrence of circumstances which probably can never again occur;" and furnished "a body of facts which can not be invalidated."

The publication of Beaumont's book was an event of great note in the medical world. Dr. S. C. Ayers of Cincinnati in a paper on the subject read before the Academy of Medicine of that city, January 1899, says: "All writers and teachers on physiology, English, French and German as well as Americans, have acknowledged their indebtedness to Beaumont for placing an obscure and doubtful subject on a well-founded basis of facts derived from his extended and critical observations;" and that "up to the present day the book is quoted, and always will be."

Dr. Beaumont afterwards lived in St. Louis, Mo., a leading man in his profession until his death in 1853. A certain street in that city bears his name to-day, while a higher and worthier tribute to his memory in that community is the Beaumont Hospital Medical College. The medical societies of Michigan (the Upper Peninsula and the State societies) have placed a memorial stone in the Mackinac fort grounds beside the old stone quarters where the surgeon dwelt when an officer of the post, and where the experiments in the case were first conducted. The inscription on the stone reads:

"Near this spot Dr. William Beaumont, U. S. A., made his experiments upon Alexis St. Martin, which brought fame to himself and honor to American medicine."

The village at that period contained about four hundred and fifty permanent inhabitants. Their chief occupation was fishing in summer and hunting in winter. The community had an antique and foreign style of its own — the Indian with his plumes and his bright and decorated costume, the Canadian rover thoughtless, bent on the present and heedless of to-morrow, and the petty trader, habituated to the woods and only temporarily in the haunts of men. The French language, or rather that known as "Canadian French," was chiefly spoken. Society was of diverse elements. The original stock was based on the old French and Indian mixture — the descendants of the canoe men and trappers and clerks and interpreters who had generally married Indian women. Gurdon Hubbard, already referred to, describing the situation as it was in the early twenties, said there were not more than twelve white women on the island, the residue of the female population being either all or part Indian. For a time during the British dominion an English element figured, but this seemed to withdraw after the island changed its sovereignty. An Irish element then appeared and continued, founding itself to some extent on intermarriage with the natives. In the flourishing period of the Fur Company the social life of the island was perhaps at its best development. It was represented by the magnates and factors of that Company, by the military circle of the fort, by the Government officials of the civil service as connected with the Custom-house and with the Indian affairs, by the company of teachers in the work of the Mission school then maintained, and by the families of the merchants and leading traders.

Like the rest of the world our island shows its changes and improvements since that day of primitive conditions. Large and luxurious steam vessels, mooring within immense dock slips, have succeeded to the canoes which once lined the pebbly shores. The picturesque wigwams and birch-bark huts and rude barrack quarters of the former "resorters" have given way to the modern hotel and boarding home and to the numerous and diversified cottages, peopled by another type of season visitors. A different class, indeed, but still the real successors are we of the Indians and of the old Fur Company trappers and boatmen who were wont to gather here, summer after summer, in the days of early Mackinac. Carriages and equipages of every description pass swiftly over roads where formerly wheeled vehicles and horses were unknown, and when dog-trains and winter sledges and a few ox carts in the hill woods comprised almost the total of animal draught power. A boulevard drive-way along the beach, designed to encircle the whole island, is in course of construction. Water works and electric lighting and the telephone system are among the present conveniences of the old-time village. The large State Park, embracing nearly one-half the woods of the island, and threaded by the best of roads, and a thing of State guardianship and care, is another modern feature. And the project of a beautiful little park, at the foot of the fort and in the current of the village life, adorned by a memorial statue of the early missionary and explorer, Marquette, whose name the park will bear, has been initiated. These are some of the changes, but in its natural beauty, its purity of atmosphere, its surrounding panorama of mighty waters, and in all that makes its subtle charm and spell, the island is the same as of yore, and beyond the power of man's enterprise to change or improve. It is a small tract of land not subject to the prevailing conditions of other communities, and to an unusual degree it preserves its pristine character.

The following, written by a reflecting visitor many years ago, when the aborigines were still lingering in the neighborhood of the island, and when modern life was in its "day of small things," may well be repeated now. The prediction it contains is seen to-day, at any rate, and doubtless will long continue to be realized: "The Straits of Mackinac will always command attention. Through this channel will pass, for ages to come, a great current of commerce, and its shores will be enlivened with civilized life where at present the Indian still lingers, but alas! is fast passing away."

CHAPTER XI

Early Mackinac had among its citizens, sparse though its population was, a number of men of strong character and great business enterprise. Among them, not to speak of all, were Michael Dousman, John Dousman, Edward Biddle, Gurdon S. Hubbard, Samuel Abbot and Ambrose Davenport. John Dousman, Abbott and Davenport were the deputation of three gentlemen referred to by Lieut. Hanks, in his report of the surrender of the fort, as having accompanied the flag of truce in the negotiations between Captain Roberts and himself. After the English came into possession, the citizens were required to take the oath of allegiance to the king. Of those then living on the island, five are reported as refusing to do this — Messrs. Davenport, Bostwick, Stone, and the two Dousmans.[1] With the exception of Michael Dousman, who was permitted to remain neutral, they were obliged to leave their homes and their property until the close of the war. Besides these, there were afterwards three men in particular who figured in large spheres, and were in reputation in other parts of the land as well as in this remote wilderness point. These were Ramsey Crooks, Robert Stuart and Henry R. Schoolcraft.

[1] Biddle and Hubbard were not then residents of the island. Biddle was a brother of Nicholas Biddle of Bank fame in Jackson's time.

Mr. Crooks came to America from Scotland, as a young man. His career was an active and stirring one. He was known in connection with the fur trade, it is said, from the Atlantic to the Pacific. His business involved much of perilous journeying and startling adventure in the north and in the far west. He

HENRY R. SCHOOLCRAFT, LL.D.

was with Hunt's expedition across the Rocky Mountains and to the Pacific coast, as far back as 1811, and again the next year he made the same overland journey back to the East. He was an educated, intelligent man, well experienced in human nature, and highly rated for his judgment, his enterprise and his integrity. He was one of Mr. Astor's right hand men in the extensive business of the fur company. In the American expedition against the island in 1814, in the attempt to dislodge the English, he, together with Davenport and John Dousman, had accompanied the squadron — the latter two as expatriated citizens, well acquainted with the waters, to help as guides; and Crooks to watch, as far as he could, the interests of Mr. Astor.[1] He did not make Mackinac his permanent residence during the whole time of his connection with the business, but was more or less on the island and engaged in its office work. New York, afterwards, was his home; and on Astor's selling out, he became chief proprietor and the president of the company. It is said of him that he concentrated, in his reminiscences, the history of the fur trade in America for forty years. He died in New York in 1859.

Robert Stuart was also a native of Scotland, born in 1784. He came to America at the age of twenty-two years, and illustrated the same spirit of enterprise and adventure. He first lived in Montreal, and served with the Northwestern Fur Co. In 1810 he connected himself, together with his uncle, David Stuart, with Mr. Astor's business, and was one of the party that sailed from New York by the ship "Tonquin" to found the fur trade city of Astoria, on the Pacific Coast. In 1812, it being exceedingly important that certain papers and dispatches be taken

[1] Schoolcraft speaking of Davenport (who, he says, was a Virginian), refers to his thus "sailing about the island and in sight of his own home." He remarks, too, that for his sufferings and losses, he ought to have been remunerated by the Government.

from Astoria to New York, and the ship in the meantime being destroyed, and there being no way of making the trip by sea, Stuart was put at the head of a party to undertake the journey overland. Ramsey Crooks was one of the band. This trip across the mountains and through the country of wild Indians, and over arid plains, involved severe hardships and peril, and illustrated the nerve, and vigor, and resources of the young leader. The party was nearly a year on the way. In 1817 he came to Mackinac and became a resident partner of the American Fur Company, and superintendent of its entire business in the west. He was remarkably energetic in business, a leader among men, and a conspicuous and forceful character wherever he might be placed. In the lack of hotel accommodations his home was constantly giving hospitable welcome and entertainment to visiting strangers. He dwelt on the island for fifteen years, and when the company sold out in 1834, removed to Detroit. He was afterward appointed by the Government as Indian Commissioner for all the tribes of the northwest, and guarded their interests with paternal care. The Indians used to speak of him as their best friend. He also served as State treasurer, and at the expiration of his term of office was trustee and secretary of the Illinois and Michigan Canal Board. Active in great commercial and public interests, he was also, subsequent to his conversion on the island in 1828, zealous and prominent in church work and always bore a high Christian character. He died very suddenly at Chicago, in 1848. His body was taken by a vessel over the lakes to Detroit for burial. In passing Mackinac the boat laid awhile at the dock, and all the people of the village paid their respects to the dead body of one who had been in former years a resident of the island, so well known and so greatly esteemed.

In connection with the Fur Company work of the island, which these two men did so much to promote, it may be well to quote from Mrs. John Kinzie, the wife of a Chicago pioneer, who with her husband was here in 1830. In her interesting book "Wau-Bun, the 'Early Day' in the Northwest," she thus writes, speaking of that period: "These were the palmy days of Mackinac. It was no unusual thing to see a hundred or more canoes of Indians at once approaching the island, laden with their articles of traffic; and if to these was added the squadron of large Mackinaw boats constantly arriving from the outposts with the furs, peltries and buffalo robes collected by the distant traders, some idea may be formed of the extensive operations and the important position of the American Fur Company, as well as of the vast circle of human beings either immediately or remotely connected with it."

Henry R. Schoolcraft lived on the island from 1833 to 1841. He was a native of the State of New York. He was a student, an investigator into the facts and phenomena of nature, a remarkable linguist, a great traveler and explorer, and a prolific writer. He was given to archæological researches; he explored the valley of the Mississippi; he investigated the mineral resources of much of the west, particularly of Missouri; and he discovered the source of the Mississippi river. His great work, and by which he is most known, was that in connection with the Indian race, having spent thirty years of his life in contact with them. Besides his travels among the tribes throughout the west and northwest, where his pursuits led him, he was the Government agent in Indian affairs, first at Sault Ste. Marie for eleven years, and then at Mackinac for eight years. He mentions that at one time over four thousand Indians were encamped along the shores of the island for a month; and that the annuities he paid that year amounted to $370,000 in money and goods. He also served in the negotiation of treaties for the Government with the tribes. While living at the Sault, he married a half-blood Indian girl. Her father, Mr. John Johnston, was an Irish gentleman of good standing, who, dwelling in the wilderness country of Lake Superior, had found a wife in the daughter of an Indian Chief. This daughter, Miss Johnston, had been sent to Europe while a young girl to be educated under the care of her father's relatives, and she became a refined and cultivated Christian lady.

Mr. Schoolcraft in his eight years' residence on the island, lived in the house known to all readers of Miss Woolson's *Anne* as the "Old Agency." He writes on his arrival: "We found ourselves at ease in the rural and picturesque grounds and domicile of the United States Agency, overhung, as it is, by impending cliffs and commanding one of the most pleasing and captivating views of lake scenery."[1] Every subject of scientific interest, all the physical phenomena of the island, and its antiquities and his-

[1] In the minds of some now living on the island he has been confused with his brother, James Schoolcraft, who also lived in the village and was murdered by a John Tanner, in 1846 — as then generally supposed.

toric features, and all questions pertaining to the Indians and their race characteristics, their habits and customs, their language, their traditions and legends, their religion, and especially all that might lead to their moral and social improvement — these were matters of his constant study. At the same time he kept abreast of the general literature of the day, reading the books of note as they appeared and himself making contributions to literature by his own books and review articles and treatises, which were published in the East and in England. In his remote island home, ice-bound for half the year and largely shut out from the world, he was yet well known by his writings in the highest circles of learning. Visitors of note from Europe as well as from the Eastern States, coming to the island, were frequently calling at his house with letters of introduction. He was voted a complimentary membership in numerous scientific, historical and antiquarian societies, both in this country and in the old world. He had correspondents among scholars and savants of the highest rank. His opinions and views on subjects of which he had made a study were greatly prized. The eminent Sir Humphrey Davy, of England, for instance, expressed the highest appreciation of certain contributions of scientific interest which Mr. Schoolcraft had prepared in his island home; and Charles Darwin, in his work, "The Descent of Man," quotes with approval some opinion he had expressed, and calls him "a most capable judge." Prof. Silliman, also ex-Presidents John Adams, Thos. Jefferson and James Madison, wrote him letters of marked approbation respecting a contribution he had written for

THE OLD AGENCY.

Built by the U. S. Government for the use of its Agent in the Indian affairs. It was both residence and office. It stood near the foot of the bluff, on the ground between the present Public School building and the well-known hotel, the Island House. The annuities to the Indians were paid at the Agency. Its spacious grounds were surrounded by palisades, and on payment days the gates were guarded by soldiers. It long survived its original purpose, but was always known as the "Old Agency." It was accidentally destroyed by fire in the winter of 1873–'74.

the American Geological Society. Bancroft conferred with him before writing those parts of his "History of the United States," which pertain to the Indians, and was in frequent correspondence with him; and Longfellow, in his Hiawatha Indian notes, expresses his sense of obligation to him. Some of Schoolcraft's lectures were translated into French, and a prize was awarded him by the National Institute of France. Among his frequent correspondents, as he was an active Christian and in sympathy with all church interests, were the secretaries of different missionary societies in the East, seeking his opinion and his counsel in reference to the location of stations and the methods of work among the Indian tribes. The amount of literary work he accomplished was remarkable, especially in view of his public services, which often required extensive journeys in distant wilderness regions, and much of camp life. He was of remarkable physical vigor and industry, however, and it is said of him, that he had been known to write from sun to sun almost every day for many years.

Mr. Schoolcraft removed from the island to New York in 1841, and after an extensive travel through Europe, devoted himself principally to literary work. He published about thirty different books. These largely pertained to his explorations, and to scientific subjects. The chief products of his pen in respect to the Indians were his "Algic Researches," and later his very extensive "Ethnological Researches among the Red Men," which was prepared under the direction and patronage of Congress. It is in six large volumes with over 300 colored engravings, and was issued in the best style of the printer's art. It is a thesaurus of information, and furnishes the most complete and authentic treatment the subject has ever received.

For nearly twenty years Mr. Schoolcraft lived at Washington, and died there in December, 1864. The Rev. Dr. Sunderland, for over forty years a Presbyterian pastor in that city, has said of him: "He was a noble Christian man, and his last years were spent in the society of his friends and among his books . . . a modest, retiring, unostentatious man, but of deep, sincere piety and greatly interested in the welfare of mankind."

CHAPTER XII

WITH the explorer, the trader and the soldier, in the early days of the French occupation, there came also the missionary. More than two centuries ago pioneer Jesuit priests planted the cross in these wilds of the upper lakes; first at Sault Ste. Marie, as early as two hundred and fifty years since, and then in 1671 in our Michilimackinac region of St. Ignace,[1] on the northern mainland, four miles across from the island. The latter work is associated particularly with Marquette, who founded it, and who was one of the most heroic and devoted of the early missionaries who came to this continent from France. He was a scholar and a man of science, according to the attainments of that day. It is said he was acquainted with six different languages. He was held in reverent esteem, both by the savages of the woods and by the traders and officers of the settlements. To his culture, his refinement and his spirituality were added the enthusiasm and daring of the explorer. He went out to find new countries as also to preach in the pagan wilds. In 1673, accompanied by Joliet, he set forth from St. Ignace with a small company in two bark canoes, on a long voyage of discovery. He struck out into Lake Michigan, thence into the rivers of Wisconsin, and thence into the Mississippi, and floated down that great river

1 Point Iroquois, as it was first known.

as far as to a point some thirty miles below the mouth of the Arkansas river, almost to the Louisiana line. There the southern journey was ended and the return trip was begun — ascending the Mississippi, entering the Illinois and thus reaching Lake Michigan again. But for Marquette the trip was never finished. He died at a point on the eastern shore of that lake, about midway between its upper and lower ends, and was buried there by his ever faithful and devoted Indian companions. Two years afterwards his body was exhumed and reverently taken back for interment at the St. Ignace Mission, which he had longingly desired again to reach, but had died without the sight. The discovery of his grave, in the present town of St. Ignace, in the year 1877, has given new interest to that locality.

Following the temporary abandonment of the French post of Michilimackinac in 1701, and the removal of the settlement to Detroit, as already referred to, the St. Ignace Mission was given up, and the church burned by the priests themselves in fear lest it should be sacrilegiously destroyed by the savages. Subsequently, on the re-establishment of the fort on the southern peninsula opposite, the Catholic mission was revived and the Church of St. Ann was organized — the church and the entire settlement of families, as well as the garrison, being within the palisade enclosure. When in 1780 the fort was removed to the island — and the settlers following — the church was also removed, its logs and timbers being taken down separately and then rejointed and set up again. It stood on the old burying lot south of the present Astor House. Subsequently it was removed to another site. An addition was made extending its length, and the old church continued to stand until it gave way to the present large edifice, built on the same spot, in 1874. As an organization, however, the church dates far back to the early days over at old Mackinaw. The ground on which the building now stands was a bequest to the parish by a Madam La Framboise, who lived near by, with the stipulation that at death her body should be buried under the altar, in case the church should be removed to the place indicated. This being done, the conditions of the will were fulfilled. This Madam was of Indian blood, and the widow of a French fur trader. She is reported to have been a woman of remarkable energy and enterprise, and on the death of her husband ably managed the business he had left. She acquired the rudiments of education after her marriage, being taught by her husband, and in later years made it a custom to receive young pupils at her house to teach them to read and write, and also to instruct them in the principles of her religion. Her daughter became the wife of Lieut. John S. Pierce, a brother of President Pierce, who was an officer at the garrison in the early days, 1815–1820.

In the early times, the island being so remote a pioneer point, and its population meagre, this parish did not always have a resident priest, and for much of the time could only be visited by one at irregular and often distant intervals. In 1782, a petition signed by merchants and other inhabitants of the village, was addressed to General Haldimand, the English Governor General of the Province, asking that the Government take steps to aid in securing a *cure,* or minister of religion, for the stated maintenance of services. There appears nothing to show that this was granted. The fur trade brought an element of population of a very mixed character. There were the educated officers and clerks of the company, and the *voyageurs* and trappers, who spent most of their time in the woods and on the water, with Mackinac as their place of resting and wage-payment, and the place of the reckless wasting of their hard-earned money. One who knew well the early character of the island, said of it, that few places on the continent had been so celebrated a locality for wild enjoyment; that the earnings of a year were often spent in the carousals of a week or a day; that the lordly Highlander, the impetuous son of Erin, and the proud and independent Englishman, did not do much better on the score of moral responsibilities than the humble *voyageurs* and *courier des bois;* that they broke generally, nine out of the ten commandments without a wince, but kept the other very scrupulously, and would flash up and call their companions to a duel who doubted them on that point!

Protestant Missions in the west gradually took shape as the settlement of the country advanced from the sea-board. The Rev. David Bacon, of the Connecticut Missionary Society, the father of the late Dr. Leonard Bacon, preached on the island for a short time as far back as 1802; not, however, establishing a mission or organizing a church. Then, in 1820, the Rev. Jedidiah Morse, D. D., a Congregational minister, the father of the inventor of the telegraph system, visited the island, and made a short stay. The same Dr. Morse was the author of "Morse's Geography," once extensively used in our schools, and still well remembered. In earlier years the fort was a chaplaincy post, and the clergyman in charge, the Rev. Mr. O'Brien, from 1842 until the opening of the civil war in 1861, conducted stated services of the Episcopal form of worship, which accommodated the people of the village as well as the soldiers. Out of this work grew the Trinity Episcopal Church, organized in 1873, under the ministration of the Rev. Wm. G. Stonex, who continued for some years the resident clergyman. For a time the parish held its Sunday services in the fort chapel; then the old Court House (now the City Hall) was used, and in 1882 the present Church building was erected. There is generally a resident clergyman in charge. The Rt. Rev. Thomas F. Davies, D. D., bishop of the diocese of Michigan, being a summer cottager, frequently officiates. The Union Congregational church was organized April 1900, and at present use the City Hall as their place of meeting. A church edifice is in contemplation.

To go back again to our earlier period. At the time of Dr. Morse's visit to the island, he was under commission by the U. S. government on a two years' tour of observation and inspection among the various Indian tribes with a view "to devise the most suitable plan to advance their civilization and happiness." [1] He arrived at the island, June 16th, in the evening, and writes of the view that greeted his eye

[1] From letter of instructions written him by John C. Calhoun, Secretary of War, Feb., 1820.

in the morning — . . . "the fort looking down from the high bluff, and a fleet of Indian canoes drawn up on the beach, along which were pitched fifty or one hundred lodges — cone-shaped bark tents — filled with three or four hundred Indians, men, women and children, come to receive their annuities from the United States Government and to trade." He remained a little over two weeks and preached in the Court House to large and attentive audiences. A week-day school and a Sabbath-school were formed for the children, and arrangements effected for Bible Society and Tract Society work. On his return to the East, the United Foreign Missionary Society, learning of the situation, took steps to plant a mission at Mackinac. The island was considered a strategic point for such operations, even as previously it had been a strategic situation from a military point of view. It was a central gathering place for the Indians for hundreds of miles away as well as from near at hand. The mission was established in 1823. The Rev. Wm. Ferry, a Presbyterian minister from the East, was appointed superintendent.

The Mission was designed chiefly as a school for the training of Indian youth. It opened with twelve pupils. The second year it numbered seventy. Two years after the opening of the enterprise the large school building and boarding house, now the hotel at the east end of the island, and bearing the original name "Mission House," was built. In 1826 the Society which had begun the work and maintained it for three years, was merged with the American Board of Commissioners for Foreign Missions. Henceforth, until it closed, the Mackinac Mission was the

REV. WM. FERRY.

MRS. FERRY.

work of that Board with headquarters in Boston. For several years the attendance at the school averaged about one hundred and fifty a year. Major Anderson, of the Canadian service, writing in 1828, says that when this mission building was erected it was thought to be large enough to accommodate all who might desire its privileges, but such was the thirst for knowledge, that the house was then full; and at least fifty more had sought admission that season who could not be received for lack of room.

Besides the rudiments of English education, the boys were taught the more useful sort of handicraft and trades, and the girls were taught sewing and housework. They were at all times under Christian influence, and were systematically instructed in the truths of the Gospel. In the Biography of Mrs. Jeremiah Porter, who before her marriage was Miss Chappelle, and who spent two years (1830–32) on the island, is given an extract from her diary, in which she speaks of visiting the Mission House and hearing the young Indian girls, at their evening lesson, repeat together the 23rd Psalm and the 55th chapter of Isaiah, and of hearing a hymn sung "by sixteen sweet Indian voices which was particularly touching." Col. Thos. McKenney, of the Indian Department, gives another interesting glimpse of the school in his book, "Sketches of a Tour to the Lakes," published in 1827. He had been sent out, the year before, from Washington as joint commissioner with General Cass in negotiating a treaty with the Indians of the North. Having touched at Mackinac he describes his calling, in company with Mr. Robert Stuart, at "the Missionary establishment in charge of Mr. Ferry." The school family were at supper, and he writes, "we joined them in their prayers, which are offered after this meal." On another day he again visited the school, and reported of it: "The buildings are admirably adapted for the object for which they were built. They are composed of a center and two wings — the center is occupied chiefly as the eating department and the offices connected therewith. The western wing accommodated the family. In the eastern wing are the school rooms, and below, in the ground story, are apartments for shoemakers and other manufactures. In the girls' school were seventy-three, from four to seventeen years old. In personal cleanliness and neatness, in behavior, in attainments in various branches, no children, white or red, excel them. The boys' school has about eighty, from four to eighteen. One is from Fond du Lac, upwards of seven hundred miles. Another from the Lake of the Woods. How far they have come to get light!" Referring to the Superintendent, Mr. Ferry, he speaks of him in terms of unqualified approbation. "Few men possess his skill, his qualification, his industry and devotion to the work. Such a pattern of practical industry is without price in such an establishment. Indeed, the entire mission family appeared to me to have undertaken this most interesting charge from the purest motives." He makes mention of Mrs. Robert Stuart as "an excellent, accomplished and intelligent lady, whose soul is in this work of mercy. This school is in her eyes, the green spot of the island. With her influence and means she has held up the hands that were ready, in the beginning of this establishment, to hang down. She looks upon Mr. Ferry and his labors as being worth more to the island than all the land of which it is composed; whilst he, with gratitude, mentions her kindness, and that of her co-operting husband."

Mrs. John Kinzie, already referred to as being on the island in 1830, visited the Mission, and in her book makes similar testimony concerning it, saying among other things: "Through the zeal and good management of Mr. and Mrs. Ferry, and the fostering encouragement of the congregation, the school was in great repute."

A church for the island soon grew out of the school. It was Presbyterian in name and form. It was a branch of Mr. Ferry's work, and he was the pastor during the whole time he remained on the island. A church building, the historic "Old Mission Church," still standing in its original dimensions and appearance, was built in 1829–30. Mackinac in those days shared with Detroit in distinction, the two towns being almost the only places of note in the State of Michigan. The Fur Company's business, together with the general trading interests which centered here, brought to the island a considerable population. Thus large and interesting congregations were furnished for this church. Besides the teachers and their families, and the pupils of the mission school, there were many families of the village, officers and clerks of the company, traders, native Indian converts and others, who were members in regular attendance. The military post, too, used to be represented — officers and men coming down the street on Sunday mornings in martial step. The soldiers would stack their guns outside in front of the church; one of the men would be detailed to stand guard over the arms, while the others would file into the pews set apart for their accommodation.

The whole number of members enrolled during the history of the church was about eighty, exclusive of the mission family. As a pioneer church on the wilderness frontier, it was remarkable in having on its membership roll, and among its office bearers as Ruling Elders, two men of such standing and public name as Robert Stuart and Henry R. Schoolcraft.

The Mackinac experiment of mission work unfortunately, was not continued long enough to show the largest results. Changes took place on the island which seriously affected the situation. It ceased to be the great resort for the Indians it had been at first. The Michigan lands were coming in demand for settlement; and the Government was deporting some of the tribes to reservations farther West. Mr. Astor retired from the Fur Company, and that business lost its former magnitude. This involved the loss of many families and a change in social conditions. In 1834, Mr. Ferry removed from the island,[1] as did Mr. Stuart, the same year. Thus, for a variety of reasons the place ceasing to be an advantageous point for the work, it was deemed best to discontinue it; and about 1836 the land (some twelve acres) and the buildings thereon were sold, and in 1837 the Mission was formally given up. During the brief history of the school, however, not less than five hundred

[1] Mr. Ferry settled at what became Grand Haven, in Michigan, himself founding the city and also its Presbyterian Church, and continued to reside there until his death in 1867.

OLD MISSION CHURCH.

children of Indian blood and habits acquired the rudiments of education, and were taught the pursuits and toils of civilized life, and many became Christians. The American Board at that time considered that the Mackinac Mission had been very successful, especially in its outreaching influence throughout the surrounding regions.

One instance of remarkable conversion in the work of the Mission, was that of an old Indian necromancer or "medicine man." His name was Wazhuska, or more popularly, Chuska. For forty years he had been famous on the island in the practice of that mysterious occultism which has often been found among low and barbarous races. He was supposed by his people to have supernatural power, and indeed the instances which have been reported of his strange facility seem remarkable. A sorcerer he might have been called, or, as such have also been designated, a "practitioner of the black art." He embraced the Christian faith with clear perception of its essential truths, and with great simplicity of spirit; and entirely renounced all his "hidden works of darkness," together with the vice of drunkenness to which he had been lamentably addicted, and after a year of testing and probation was admitted to membership in the Mission Church. He died in 1837, and was buried on Round Island. This story of Chuska and his conversion by the power of divine grace, was considered of such interest that we find it related by Schoolcraft in three of his books — his "Personal Memoirs," his "Oneota" (a collection of miscellany which tells of Chuska under the heading "The Magician of the Manitouline Islands"), and in his elaborate six volume work published by act of Congress. In his account of the case as given in the last named publication he furnishes representations of the crude pictographic charms, and totems and symbols, which Chuska was accustomed to use in his pagan incantations, and which at the time of his conversion he had surrendered to Mr. Schoolcraft. The tale of Chuska is also told by Mrs. Jameson in the narrative of her visit to Mackinac in 1837; and in Strickland's "Old Mackinaw."

The Mission given up, the school closed, the teachers and their families gone, the trade and emporium character of the village falling away, the church organization did not long survive. There was no successor of Mr. Ferry in the pastorate. Mr. Schoolcraft, as an office bearer in the church, and always actively interested in its welfare, did all that a layman, so fully occupied as he, could do for its maintenance, often conducting a Sabbath service and reading a sermon to the people from some good collection. But so largely losing its families by removal, and unable under existing conditions to secure a pastor, the church organization became extinct. The church building, however, the "Old Mission Church" as it is familiarly known to this day, has survived for sixty years the lapse of the organization. It is probably the oldest Protestant Church structure in the whole Northwest. And while other ancient church buildings have been enlarged and changed in the course of years; and extension put on, or a front or a tower added, or other material alterations made; this one, from end to end, and in its entire structural form, remains the same as at the time of its early dedication. It has stood four square to all the winds that have blown, as "solid as the faith of those who built it,"[1] unchanged from its original style and its bare and simple appearance, with its old weather-vane and its wonderfully bright tin-topped belfry — a mute memorial of a most worthy history of two generations ago. Despite its disuse and its increasing dilapidation, it has long been an object of tender interest, and has been visited by hundreds every season. It is gratifying, therefore, to know that a number of the summer cottagers and other visitors, joined by some of the island residents, have purchased the old church, and repaired and restored it so as to present the old-time appearance in which it had been known for well nigh seventy years.[2] The gray weather-worn exterior is purposely left unpainted. The same old "high-up" pulpit, the plain square pews with doors on them, the diminutive panes of glass in the windows, the quaint old-fashioned gallery at the entrance end — all these features appear as at the first. The property is held in trust for the purchasers by a board of seven trustees, five of whom are to be visitors who own or rent cottages, and two to be residents of the village. There is no ecclesiastical organization in connection with the building, nor any denominational color or control. The motive in the movement has been, first, to preserve the old sanctuary as a historic relic of the island and memorial of early mission work; and, second, to use it as a chapel for union religious services during the few weeks when summer tourists crowd the island.

1 Miss Woolson's "*Anne.*"
2 Repaired and restored in 1895.

CHAPTER XIII

Our Island in its dimensions is three miles east and west, and two miles north and south. It has a crescent shaped harbor, which gives the same outline to the village nestling on the rounded beach. There can be few places so small and circumscribed that can furnish so many pleasing impressions. In its antiquarian interest, in its unlikeness to the outside world, in its dim traditions, and in its entrancing charms of natural scenery, there is found every variety for the eye, the taste and the imagination. While small enough to steam around it in an hour on the excursion boats, it is yet large enough to admit of long secluded walks through its quiet, gentle woods. In the three score years or more that visitors have been coming here, there have grown up for it such tributes and terms of admiration as, Gem of the Straits, Fairy Isle, Tourists' Paradise, Princess of the Islands, and such like.

Rising almost perpendicularly out of the water, one hundred and fifty feet high, with its white stone cliffs and bluffs, and twice that height back on the crest of the hill, and covered with the densest and greenest foliage, it is an object of sight for many miles in every direction. Throughout we find that development and variety of beauty which nature makes when left to herself. The trees are the maple, and pine, and birch, and old beeches with strait and far-reaching branches and with rugged trunks, on which can be seen initials and dates running back many years — the mementos of visitors of long ago. The hardy cedar abounds also, and the evergreen spruce, larch and laurel, and tamarack. Throughout the woods running in different directions, are winding roads, arched and shaded by the overhanging tree-

ARCH ROCK.

tops, as if they were continuous bowers, and bewitching footpaths and trails; the fragrance of the fir and the balsam is everywhere, and a buoyancy in the atmosphere which invites to walking — the whole tract being safe, always, for even children to wander in. You come upon patches of the delicate wild strawberry with its aromatic flavor, the wild rose, the blue gentian, profuse beds of daisies, said to be of the largest variety in America, the curious "Indian pipes," luxuriant ferns in dark nooks, forever hidden from the sun, and thickest coverings of moss on rocks and old tree trunks. Then always, from every quarter and in every direction, are to be seen the great waters of the lakes, so many "seas of sweet water," as they were described by Cadillac, the early French commander in this region — Huron to the east and Michigan on the west, with the Mackinac Straits between, and all so deep, so pure, so beautifully colored; and whether in the dead calm, when smooth as a floor, or shimmering and glistening in the sunshine, or in the silvery sheen of the moon at night, or again tossing and billowing in the storm — always exercising the power of a spell upon the beholder. Ever in sight, too, are the neighboring islands, standing out in the midst as masses of living green; and the light-houses with their faithful, friendly night work; and the young cities on the two mainlands in opposite directions; and always the picturesque old fort. Then, scattered over the islands are glens, and dells, and springs, and fantastic rock formations, ("rock-osities" they were sometimes facetiously called in early days). Many of these formations are interesting in a geological point of view as well as for their marked appearance and their legendary associations; and two of them, Sugar Loaf and Arch Rock, have been much studied by scientists, and are pictured in certain college text books to illustrate the teachings of natural science.

On the eastern part of the island you come on certain openings which the earlier French termed *Grands Jardins.* Schoolcraft says no resident pretended to

A MODERN MACKINAC GARDEN.

know their origin; that they had evidently been cleared for tilling purposes at a very early day, and that in his time there were mounds of stones, in a little valley near Arch Rock, which resembled the Scotch cairns, and which he supposes were the stones gathered out in the preparation of these little fields. These openings continued, at times, to be utilized for planting purposes to a period within the memory of persons now living on the island. For a long time past, however, they have been left alone, and nature has beautifully adorned them with a very luxuriant and graceful growth of evergreen trees and parterres of juniper in self-arranged grouping and order, making each such place appear as if laid out and cultivated on the most artistic plans of landscape gardening.

For summer comfort — that is, for the escape of heat and the enjoyment of sifted, clean, delicious air — there can be no place excelling. As an old-time frequenter once said of it: "It must be air that came from Eden and escaped the curse." The immense bodies of water in the necklace of lakes thrown about the island become the regulator of its temperature. The only complaint that visitors ever make of the climate, is that it is not quite warm enough, and that blankets can not be "put away for the summer," but are in nightly requisition, and that the "family hearthstone" claims July and August as part of its working season. Malaria and hay fever are unknown. Dr. Daniel Drake, of Cincinnati, an eminent medical authority in his day, thus wrote from the island: "To one of jaded sensibilities, all around him is refreshing. A feeling of security comes over him, and when, from the rocky battlements of Fort Mackinac, he looks down upon the surrounding wastes, they seem a mount of defense against the host of annoyances from which he has sought refuge — the historic associations, not less than the scenery of the island, being well fitted to maintain the salutary mental excitement." [1]

The island has its legends, and folk-lore, and traditionary tales of romance and tragedy. There is not so much of this, however, as many suppose. It is small in area and its scope for scenes, and tales, and associations is limited. Reference has already been made to Arch Rock as the gateway of entrance, in the Indian mind, for their Manitou of the lakes, when he visited the island, and to Sugar Loaf as his fancied wigwam, and to other rock formations which towered above the ground and were personified into watching giants. The Devil's Kitchen, on the southwest beach, has also been mentioned, but as divested of all mystery and association with the dim and early past. Chimney Rock and Fairy Arch are but appropriate names for interesting natural objects. The lofty, jutting cliff known as Pontiac's Look-out, is undoubtedly an admirable look-out spot, and is often so used now, as it probably often was in the days of Indian strifes when canoes of war parties went to and fro over the waters of the Straits. But we can not vouch for its ever having been *Pontiac's* watch-tower.

[1] "*Treatise on the Principal Diseases of North America,*" p. 348.

"Hygeia, too, should place her temple here; for it has one of the purest, driest, cleanest and most healthful atmospheres." —*Schoolcraft.*

For although the influence of that chieftain was felt in these remote parts, his home was near Detroit; and while we read of his traveling to the East and the South, and as having had part in the battle of Braddock's defeat near Pittsburgh, we find nothing to show that he had ever been so far north as our island, or at least had ever sojourned there. Lover's Leap, rising abruptly 145 feet above the lake, is too good a pinnacle, and too suitable for such sadly romantic purpose, as far as precipitous height and frightful rocks beneath are concerned, not to have suggested the tale of the too faithful, heart-sore Indian maiden. The story of Skull Cave has already been told; and although a piece of history, as far as the name of Henry the trader figures in it, should be justly regarded with as much interest as if it belonged to myth and fable. But at the same time, with all the modifications which a sober realism may demand, there is begotten in the mind of everyone who breathes the soft and dreamy air, and surrenders himself to the witchery of the little island, an im-

CHIMNEY ROCK.

pression of the weird, and the mystical, and the poetic, however little defined and embodied it may be. This impression is increased in the sense of charm imparted by the dim and shadowy past of a noble but untutored race of nature's children in connection with a spot of such rare attractiveness, and which, dissimilar in formation and character from all the other

SUGAR LOAF.

land about, seems as though it were separate from the ordinary seats of life.

Arch Rock has long been celebrated. It appears as if hanging in the air, and as a caprice of nature. It is a part of the precipitous cliff-side, and stands a hundred and forty feet above the water's edge. It has been accounted for by the more rapid decomposition of the lower than of the upper parts of the calcareous stone bank — which process, however, it used to be thought, was fast extending to the whole. McKenney in his "Tour of the Lakes," published in 1827, thus writes: "This arch is crumbling, and a few years will deprive the island of Michilimackinac of a curiosity which it is worth visiting to see, even if this were the only inducement." The latter remark is most true, but we are glad he was so mistaken in the first part of his sentence. The arch has survived the unfortunate prophecy for seventy years, and bids fair still to hold on. It is true, however, that some portions may have fallen, and the surface of the cross-way been reduced, since the days when boys played on it, and when, according to an early tradition, a lady rode horse-back over the span.

Sugar Loaf is another curiosity in stone; conical in shape, like the old-fashioned form in which hard, white sugar used to be prepared. Including the plateau out of which it rises, it is two hundred and eighty-four feet high, erect and rugged, in appearance somewhat between a pyramid of Egypt and an obelisk. Like the Arch, it is a "survival of the fittest"— the softer substance about it being worn away and carried off in the process of geological changes, and leaving it solitary among the trees.

Robinson's Folly is the lofty, broad and blunt precipitous cliff at the East end of the island, one hundred and twenty-seven feet above the beach. The origin of the name is uncertain, save that it is associated in some way with the English Captain Robertson (Robinson) who belonged to the fort garrison for seven years, and, as already mentioned, was its commandant from 1782 to 1787. There are no less than five traditionary stories, or legends, in explanation of the name. These stories vary from the prosaic and trifling, to the very romantic and tragical. A common account is that he built a little bower house on the very edge of the cliff which he made a place of resort, and revelry mayhap, in summer days; and that once, either by a gale of wind or by the crumbling of the outer ledge of stone, the house fell to the beach below. One version of the legend has Robinson himself in the house at the time, and, like a devoted sea captain "going down with his ship," dashed to death in the fall. Another is that on one occasion when a feast and carousal were projected on the cliff, and when the things of good cheer were all in readiness, and the participants, led by their host, delaying for a little their arrival, some lurking Indians, watchful and very hungry, stole a march on the company and devoured all that was in sight.

The other tales are of a different hue. One is, that once walking near this spot the Captain thought he saw just before him, and gazing at him, a beautiful maiden. On his attempting gallantly to approach her, she kept receding, and walking backwards as she moved she came dangerously near the edge. As he rushed forward to her rescue, the girl proved to be but a phantom and dissolved into thin air, while the impetuous captain was dashed to death on the rocks below. Yet another is of this order: That Robertson (Robinson) had been one of the garrison force at the old fort across the Straits at the time of the massacre in 1763, and had been saved by an Indian girl who was exceedingly attached to him. After removing to the island, and bringing a white bride

ROBINSON'S FOLLY.

A large ledge formerly projected from the top of this cliff, overhanging the beach and commanding a view of the lake and the surrounding islands. On that ledge it is probable the fateful summer house had been erected. In course of time this projecting part broke and fell to the beach below. The rocks to-day seen at the base are doubtless some of the fragments. The whole of the crag did not sheer off at once, as an old drawing, made in 1839, shows a portion still remaining.

there, the Indian girl followed him and dwelt in a lodge he had built for her on the brow of the great cliff, nursing her jealousy and revenge. She begged one last interview with him before leaving the place forever. On the Captain's granting this, and standing beside her on the edge, she suddenly seized his arm in her frenzy and leaped off, dragging him with her to death.

There is one more of this harrowingly tragical kind, in the attempt to explain the naming, which had much currency in earlier days, and is given in tourists' notes of sixty years ago: That Robinson had married an amiable and attractive Indian girl, Wintemoyeh, the youngest daughter of Peezhicki, a great war chief of the Chippewas, and had brought her to his home at the fort. This aroused the deadly hatred of Peezhicki, who had reserved the girl for one of the warriors of his tribe. Robinson celebrated his marriage by giving a banquet feast in his bower on the cliff. The bride was present, and a company of guests. The father learned of the feast and concealed himself in the cedar bushes to shoot the man who had taken his daughter. A faithful sergeant, (the story even gives his name, MacWhorter), was present and saw the Indian level his gun. He sprang up to protect the Captain, and himself received the shot and fell dead. Robinson then grappled with the fierce chief, and in the struggle the two men came dangerously near the brow. The Indian, with his tomahawk raised, took a step or two backward to get better poise for his blow. This brought him to the very edge. A piece of stone gave way and he fell, but saved himself by catching at the projecting root of a tree. The girl now seeing her husband safe and only her father in danger, sprang forward to his help. He was thus able to raise himself to where she stood. Then seizing her around the waist, he dashed off from the cliff and both perished together.

The first two of these stories concerning the famous cliff, might very naturally suggest the name "Folly." But the others smack more of profound tragedy, spiced with romance. Of course, Robinson was not in the massacre affair of long before, across the straits; he being at that time in army service, under Gen. Bouquet, against the Indians in Eastern Pennsylvania. That he met his death on the island by falling over the cliff, or even in a more normal manner, is a supposition only, without any evidence. There is reason to suppose he still "lived to fight another day" after leaving the island post. It may be added, too, that at the period of his Mackinac command he had already seen over thirty years of service in the English army, and was no longer in the romance and lively heyday of youth. There must, however, have been something about a summer bower or hut, and something about feasting, and something about a dreadful fall, which illustrated the "folly" of establishing a pleasure resort on the very brow of a dreadful precipice. Viewed together, these stories all become interesting as throwing some light on the origin of myths, and as showing how traditions, exceedingly variant, may yet have some of the same threads running through them all. But I would not philosophize. I simply rehearse these stories, the trivial and the grave, and leave them to the imagination and the choice of the reader.

CHAPTER XIV

From an early day the island's charm of sylvan and water scenery and its delightful summer air, together with its historical associations and its flavor of antiquity, gave it a wide-spread fame. There are but few places anywhere in our country that are older as tourist resorts. Seventy and eighty years ago visitors were coming here, despite the difficulty and tedium in that time, of reaching so remote a point. Persons of high distinction in public life and in the walks of literature, and travelers from foreign countries, were often among the visitors; and our island has figured in many descriptive books of travel. As some of these authors wrote so appreciatingly of the island, and as those particular books of long ago are now out of print and not easily accessible, I think the readers of this sketch will be pleased to see a few extracts. These writers all speak of having known the island by reputation in advance of their coming, and of being drawn by its fame.

In 1843, the Countess Ossoli, better known as our American Margaret Fuller, of Boston, spent nine days in Mackinac, as part of a protracted journey she made in the northwest, and which she detailed in her book, " Summer on the Lakes." She expressed in advance her pleasurable anticipation of " the most celebrated beauties of the island of Mackinac; " and then adds her tribute to "the exceeding beauty of the spot and its position." She arrived at a time when nearly two thousand Indians (and "more coming every day") were encamped on the beach to receive their annual payments from the government. As the vessel came into the harbor "the Captain had some rockets let off which greatly excited the Indians, and their wild cries resounded along the shores." The island was "a scene of ideal loveliness, and these wild forms adorned it as looking so at home in it." She represents it as a "pleasing sight, after the raw, crude, staring assemblage of houses everywhere sure to be met in this country, to see the old French town, mellow in its coloring, and with the harmonious effect of a slow growth which assimilates naturally with objects around it." Concerning Arch Rock, she says: "The arch is perfect, whether you look up through it from the lake, or down through it to the transparent waters." She both ascended and descended "the steep and crumbling path, and rested at the summit

LESLIE AVE.

beneath the trees, and at the foot upon the cool mossy stones beside the lapsing wave." Sugar Loaf rock struck her as having "the air of a helmet, as seen from an eminence at the side. The rock may be ascended by the bold and agile. Half way up is a niche to which those, who are neither, can climb a ladder." The woods she describes as "very full in foliage, and in August showed the tender green and pliant life of June elsewhere." She gives us a view from the bluffs on the harbor side: "I never wished to see a more fascinating picture. It was an hour of the deepest serenity; bright blue and gold with rich shadows. Every moment the sunlight fell more mellow. The Indians were grouped and scattered among the lodges; the women preparing food over the many small fires; the children, half naked, wild as little goblins, were playing both in and out of the water; bark canoes upturned upon the beach, and others coming, their square sails set and with almost arrowy speed." And a familiar picture is this: "Those evenings we were happy, looking over the old-fashioned garden, over the beach, and the pretty island opposite, beneath the growing moon."

A two-volume book (published anonymously and giving no clue to its author, except that he was a practicing physician of New York City), titled "Life on the Lakes, or a Trip to the Pictured Rocks," describes a visit to Mackinac in 1835.[1] "Though the first glance," he says, "at any looked for object is most always disappointing, it is not so when you first see Mackinac." A moonlight

[1] The author is supposed to have been Dr. Chandler R. Gilman, of the College of Physicians and Surgeons, New York.

view of the island from the waters, he thus describes: "The scene was enchanting; the tall white cliff, the whiter fort, the winding, yet still precipitous pathway, the village below buried in a deep, gloomy shade, the little bay where two or three small, half-rigged sloops lay asleep upon the water." It reminded him of descriptions he had read of Spanish scenery, "where the white walls of some Moorish castle crown the brow of the lofty Sierra." In describing his stay on the island he makes interesting mention of a Sunday service he attended at the Old Mission Church. He reports the building as neat and commodious, though the congregation was small. There was no Protestant clergyman on the island, but Mr. Schoolcraft (the ruling elder of the church) conducted the service and read from some book a very good sermon. The singing of the choir was excellent, and was led by a sergeant of the fort. The whole appearance of the congregation, he thought, was very striking; officers and privates of the garrison, with the marks of rank of the one class, and the plainer uniforms of the other, were mingled together in the body of the church; there were well-dressed ladies and gentlemen of the village along with those of simpler attire; and here and there were Indians wearing blankets, and standing about the doors were others of that race in their ordinary savage dress.

He mentions in evident astonishment, and as conveying a hint about the island climate, his eating cherries and currants in Mr. Schoolcraft's garden in the month of September. And as a piece of harmless pleasantry, we may yet give another of his observations of sixty-two years ago: "There are more cows in Mackinac than in any other place of its size in the known world, and every cow has at least one bell."

English visitors in their tours of observation through the United States were often drawn thither — making the long journey to these upper lakes, and stopping off to see the island of whose fame they had heard. Captain Marryatt, first an officer of celebrity in the English navy, but more known in this country as a novelist largely given to sea tales, was here in the summer of 1837. In his "Diary of America" he writes of Mackinac: "It has the appearance of a fairy island floating on the water, which is so pure and transparent that you may see down to almost any depth, and the air above is as pure as the water that you feel invigorated as you breathe it.[1] The first reminiscence brought to my mind after I had landed was the description by Walter Scott of the island and residence of Magnus Troil and his daughters Minna and Brenda, in the novel, 'The Pirate.'" The appearance of the village streets, largely given to sails, cordage, nets, fish barrels and the like, still further suggested the resemblance to his mind, and he says he might have imagined himself "transferred to that Shetland Isle, had it not been for the lodges of the Indians on the beach, and the Indians themselves, either

[1] Marryatt's admiration of the transparent waters suggests what I find related of a certain lady of long ago, that once sailing in the harbor and gazing with rapt fondness into the pellucid depths, she enthusiastically exclaimed: "Oh, I could wish to be drowned in these pure, beautiful waters!"

running about or lying on the porches before the whisky stores."

There were also two lady visitors here from England, in the days of early Mackinac: Mrs. Jameson and Miss Harriet Martineau. Both have high rank and distinction in English literature. Each of them published her impressions of Mackinac after returning home. In their admiration and enthusiasm for the island they could not be surpassed by the most devoted American visitor who ever touched these shores.

Mrs. Jameson is well known as the writer of such books as "Sacred and Legendary Art," "Legends of the Madonna," "Essays of Art, Literature and Social Morals," "Memoirs of the Early Italian Painters," etc. Miss Martineau was of more vigorous intellect, and her writings deal more with subjects of political economy and social philosophy. She it was, too, who translated and introduced into England the writings of the French philosopher Comte. As both these books which touch on Mackinac, written over sixty years ago, were descriptive of travels, and not of the same general interest which attaches to their other writings, they are now out of print and have become rare.

Mrs. Jameson's visit was in the summer of 1837. She came up Lake Huron from Detroit by steamboat, and arrived in the harbor at early dawn. She thus describes her first view of the island as she had it from the deck of the vessel: "We were lying in a tiny bay, crescent-shaped. On the east the whole sky was flushed with a deep amber glow flecked with softest shadows of rose color, the same splendor reflected in the lake; and between the glory above and the glory below stood the little missionary church, its light spire and belfry defined against the sky." She speaks of the "abrupt and picturesque heights robed in richest foliage," and of the "little fortress, snow-white and gleaming in the morning light;" of an encampment of Indian wigwams, ("picturesque dormitories," she calls them) up and down the beach on the edge of the lake which, "transfused and unruffled, reflected every form as in a mirror, . . . an elysian stillness and balmy serenity enwrapping the whole." And, again, we hear her speaking of "the exceeding beauty of this little paradise of an island, the attention which has been excited by its enchanting scenery, and the salubrity of its summer climate."

Mrs. Jameson made quite an extended stay at Mackinac, the guest of Mr. and Mrs. Schoolcraft, at their home in the Old Agency—"The house embowered in foliage, the ground laid out in gardens, the gate opening on the very edge of the lake." She pictures Mrs. Schoolcraft with "features decidedly Indian, accent slightly foreign, a soft, plaintive voice, her language pure and remarkably elegant, refined, womanly and unaffectedly pious." She saw the island throughout, taking tramps over it and "delicious drives," and writes of it as "wonderfully beautiful—a perpetual succession of low, rich groves, alleys, green dingles and bosky dales." After her glowing description, she sums up by saying, "It is a bijou of an island. A little bit of fairy ground, just such a thing as some of our amateur travelers would like to pocket and run away with (if they could) and set down in the midst of their fish ponds; skull-cave, wigwams, Indians and all."

Miss Martineau spent two years in this country, traveling extensively through the States and writing her impressions. She published two books as the outcome of this journeying, "Society in America," and afterwards, her "Retrospect of Western Traveling." It was in July, 1836, that she visited Mackinac, and it is in the first named of these two books that she tells of it. She came by way of Lake Michigan, from Chicago, traveling in a slow-going sail-vessel, and approaching the island in the evening towards sun-setting time. As did Mrs. Jameson, so Miss Martineau first pictures it as viewed from the vessel: "We saw a white speck before us; it was the barracks of Mackinaw, stretching along the side of its green hills, and clearly visible before the town came into view. The island looked enchanting as we approached, as I think it always must, though we had the advantage of seeing it first steeped in the most golden sunshine that ever hallowed lake or shore."

The day of her arrival was the 4th of July, and, "The colors were up on all the little vessels in the harbor. The national flag streamed from the garrison. The soldiers thronged the walls of the barracks; half-breed boys were paddling about in their canoes, in the transparent waters; the half-French, half-Indian population of the place were all abroad in their best. An Indian lodge was on the shore, and a picturesque dark group stood beside it. The cows were coming down the steep green slope to the milking. Nothing could be more bright and joyous."

Describing the appearance of the village, she took note of some of the old French houses, "dusky and roofed with bark. The better houses stand on the first of the three terraces which are distinctly marked. Behind them are swelling green knolls; before them gardens sloping down to the narrow slip of white beach, so that the grass seems to grow almost into the clear rippling waves. There were two small piers with little barks alongside, and piles of wood for the steamboats. Some way to the right stood the quadrangle of missionary buildings, and the white missionary church. Still further to the right was a shrubby precipice down to the lake; and beyond, the blue waters."

She did not leave the vessel that evening, but some of the party having met the commandant of the fort, an engagement was made for an early walk in the morning. So they were up and ashore at five o'clock, and under the escort of the officer they took in the beauties of the hill and the woods. And thus she tells us of it: "No words can give an idea of the charms of this morning walk. We wound about in a vast shrubbery, with ripe strawberries under foot, wild flowers all around, and scattered knolls and opening vistas tempting curiosity in every direction." Coming suddenly on Arch Rock, which she calls the "Natural Bridge of Mackinaw," she is "almost struck backwards" by the grandeur—"the horizon line of the lake falling behind the bridge, and the blue expanse of waters filling the entire arch; shrubbery tufting the sides and dangling from the bridge, the soft, rich hues in which the whole was dressed seeming borrowed from the autumn sky."

But especially charming and impressive, she thought, was the prospect from Fort Holmes. As she looked out on the glassy lake and the green tufted islands, she compares it to what Noah might have seen the first bright morning after the deluge. "Such a cluster of little paradises rising out of such a congregation of waters. Blue waters in every direction, wholly unlike any aspect of the sea, cloud shadows and specks of white vessels. Bowery islands rise out of it; bowery promontories stretch down into it; while at one's feet lies the melting beauty which one almost fears will vanish in its softness before one's eyes; the beauty of the shadowy dells and sunny mounds, with browsing cattle and springing fruit and flowers. Thus, would I fain think, did the world emerge from the flood."

After their early walk, Miss Martineau and her party took breakfast with the courteous commandant at one of the old stone quarters of the fort, and sat a while on the piazza overlooking the village and the harbor. In response to her inquiries about the healthfulness and the climate, the officer humorously replied that it was so healthy people had to get off the island to die; and that as to the climate, they had nine months winter and three months cool weather.

The sailing vessel on which the party were passengers was bound for Detroit, and the Captain had already overstayed his time. So they had to leave that same day.[1] In reference to her departure she writes: "We were in great delight at having seen Mackinaw, at having the possession of its singular imagery for life. But this delight was dashed with the sorrow of leaving it. I could not have believed how deeply it is possible to regret a place, after so brief an acquaintance with it." And then she tells how she did, just what thousands since have done, who after visiting the island have regretfully sailed away from it: "We watched the island as we rapidly receded. Its flag first vanished; then its green terraces and slopes, its white barracks, and dark promontories faded, till the whole disappeared behind a headland and light-house of the Michigan shore."

We close Miss Martineau's tribute with this comprehensive note of admiration: "From place to place in my previous traveling, I had been told of the charms of the lakes, and especially of the Island of Mackinaw. This island is chiefly known as a principal station of the great Northwestern Fur Company. Others know it as the seat of an Indian Mission. Others, again, as a frontier garrison. It is known to me as the wildest and tenderest piece of beauty that I have yet seen on God's earth."

Captain Marryatt, who had read this description before his visit to the island (already referred to) said, when writing his own impressions, "Miss Martineau has not been too lavish in her praises of Mackinaw." These testimonies by persons of wide

[1] Schoolcraft in his journal makes note of her calling at his house that morning, and of her expressing "an enthusiastic admiration for the natural beauties of Michilimackinac.

travel, and of cultivated taste and power of observation, and visitors as they were from another land, come down to us very pleasantly from those far gone days.

BIBLIOGRAPHY

Michigan Pioneer and Historical Collections.
Wisconsin Historical Collections.
Hennepin's Narrative, Edited by Shea.
Baron La Hontan's New Voyages to North America.
Charlevoix' Account of Voyage to Canada.
Alexander Henry's Travels.
Capt. Jonathan Carver's Travels Through the Canadas.
Heriot's Travels Through the Canadas.
Isaac Weld's Travels Through the States of North America and Provinces of Canada.
Schoolcraft's Works.
Drake's Indians of the North-west.
Catlin's North American Indians.
Parkman's Works.
Sir Alexander Mackenzie's Voyages, with Account of the Fur Trade.
Beckles Willson's The Great Company.
H. H. Robinson's The Great Fur Land.
Washington Irving's Astoria.
Herbert H. Bancroft's The North-west Coast, in his History of the Pacific States.
Henry Adams' History of the United States.
Rogers' Concise Account of North America.
John Adams' Works.
Whitelock's Life of Jay.
American State Papers.
Winsor's The Mississippi Basin.
McAfee's History of the Late War in the Western Country.
Chas. J. Ingersoll's Sketch of the Second War.
Davison's Sketches of War of 1812.
Robert Christie's War of 1812.
Lossing's Field-book of War of 1812.
Holmes' American Annals.
Palmer's Historical Register.
Kingsford's History of Canada.
Boudinot's Canada.
Robert's History of Canada.

Hinsdale's Old North-west.
Moore's The North-west under Three Flags.
Tuttle's History of Michigan.
Sheldon's Early History of Michigan.
McKenney's Tour to the Lakes.
Colton's Tour of the American Lakes.
Life on the Lakes, or a Trip to the Pictured Rocks. Anonymous.
Disturnell, A Trip Through the Lakes of North America.
Harriet Martineau's Society in America.
Mrs. Jameson's Winter Studies and Summer Rambles.
Capt. Marryatt's Diary in America.
Margaret Fuller's Summer on the Lakes.
Strickland's Old Mackinaw.
Van Fleet's Old and New Mackinaw.
Bailey's Mackinac, Formerly Michilimackinac.
Kelton's, The Annals of Fort Mackinac.
Cook's Old Fort Drummond.
Dr. Wm. Beaumont's Experiments and Observations on the Gastric Juice.
Dr. Drake's Treatise on the Principal Diseases of North America.
Gurdon Hubbard's Autobiography.
Mrs. John Kinzie's Wau-Bun, the "Early Day" in the North-west.
Life of Rev. Jedidiah Morse, D.D.
Rev. John H. Pitezel's Light and Shadows of Missionary Life.

We at Avery Color Studios thank you for purchasing this book. We hope it has provided many hours of enjoyable reading.

Learn more about Michigan and the Great Lakes area through a broad range of titles that cover mining and logging days, early Indians and their legends, Great Lakes shipwrecks, Cully Gage's Northwoods Readers (full of laughter and occasional sadness), and full-color pictorials of days gone by and the natural beauty of this land.

Also available are beautiful full-color placemats and note stationery.

To obtain a free catalog, please call (800) 722-9925 in Michigan, or (906) 892-8251, or tear out this page and mail it to us. Please tape or staple the card and put a stamp on it.

PLEASE RETURN TO:

Avery Color Studios
Star Route - Box 275
Au Train, Michigan 49806
Phone: (906) 892-8251
IN MICHIGAN
CALL TOLL FREE
1-800-722-9925

Your complete shipping address:

____

____

____

____

Fold, Staple, Affix Stamp and Mail

____

____

____

____

Avery COLOR STUDIOS
Star Route - Box 275
AuTrain, Michigan 49806